OVERLOAD

OVERLOAD

Finding the Truth in Today's Deluge of News

Bob Schieffer

with

H. Andrew Schwartz

CSIS | CENTER FOR STRATEGIC &
INTERNATIONAL STUDIES

ROWMAN & LITTLEFIELD
Lanham • Boulder • New York • London

Published by Rowman & Littlefield
An imprint of The Rowman & Littlefield Publishing Group, Inc.
4501 Forbes Boulevard, Suite 200, Lanham, Maryland 20706
www.rowman.com

6 Tinworth Street, London SE11 5AL, United Kingdom

British Library Cataloguing in Publication Information Available

Library of Congress Cataloging-in-Publication Data

Names: Schieffer, Bob author. | Schwartz, H. Andrew author.
Title: Overload : finding the truth in today's deluge of news / Bob Schieffer with H. Andrew Schwartz.
Description: Lanham : Rowman & Littlefield, 2017. | Includes index.
Identifiers: LCCN 2017021959 (print) | LCCN 2017034151 (ebook) | ISBN 9781538107225 (Electronic) | ISBN 9781538107218 (cloth : alk. paper) | ISBN 9781538131053 (paper : alk. paper)
Subjects: LCSH: Journalism—Political aspects—United States—History—21st century. | Mass media—Political aspects—United States—History—21st century. | Press and politics—United States.
Classification: LCC PN4888.P6 (ebook) | LCC PN4888.P6 S35 2017 (print) | DDC 070.4/49320973—dc23
LC record available at https://lccn.loc.gov/2017021959

The scarcest resource in journalism now is attention span. We used to live in a world governed by the laws of physics, time and space—time on the air, space in a newspaper—were our key constraints. The really controlling force in the world right now is how long can you keep your audience, your followers, consuming the journalism you create.

—Michael Oreskes, NPR

Contents

Foreword   xi

Part I   How We Got from There to Here   1

1. Are We Getting the Right Stuff?   3

2. The Challenge of Campaign 2016:
How Do You Solve a Problem Like the Donald?   13

3. The Numbers Guys: What the Pollsters Missed   21

4 And That's the Way It Is, er, Was:
Newspapers, Gatekeepers, and a More Orderly Time   25

5. And Here's the Way We Are:
New Neighbors in the News Neighborhood   37

6. Fake News: A Clear and Present Danger   51

Part II The Future Has Arrived   63

7. Walt Mossberg: Bridging the Gap   65

8. The *Washington Post*: New Culture, New Ways   71

9. The *New York Times*:
Doing What They Do Best (but Faster)   79

10. The *Wall Street Journal*:
Separating Church and State   85

11. The *Texas Tribune*: Filling a Texas-Size Void   91

12. Island in the Stream: CBS News Goes Digital   97

13. Andy Lack: Around the World and Back for More   103

14. The Cable Guy(s)   107

15. The Root: Straight Talk and a Little Shade   115

16. The Year of Living Righteously:
NPR Gets Back to Basics   119

17. Podcast News: The Rebirth of Cool   123

18. Newsletters: So Old They're New   137

19. Stephen Colbert: The Case of the Stolen Gig   141

20. Flying Solo Sooner:
Training Reporters for the New Era   147

Part III Final Thoughts 155

21. 2016: Reflections on the Year That Was   157

Afterword   171

Acknowledgments   187

Index   189

About the Authors and Contributors   201

About the Center for Strategic & International Studies   203

Foreword

NOT SINCE THE NIXON ADMINISTRATION when Spiro Agnew called them "nattering nabobs of negativity" have reporters seen their integrity challenged with such reckless ferocity as during the first weeks of the Trump administration. From his White House podium, the new president regularly called them "dishonest," purveyors of "fake news," and finally "enemy of the American people."

His senior advisor Stephen K. Bannon called them "the opposition party" and told them to shut up.

Although it never stooped to such name-calling, the Clinton campaign and its surrogates kept up a daily barrage of press criticism throughout the campaign. Other criticism came from beyond the campaign organizations and sometimes from within the profession.

This book is not meant as a rebuttal, nor does it take exception to the right of any and all to criticize the press. That is as much a part of free speech as the right to publish. Rather, this is a series of chapters that examines journalism and those who practice it—how they see their profession, how it has been changed by new technology, and how well they believe they are carrying out their responsibility to provide Americans with the information they need to be good citizens. It is also an attempt to help those outside the profession to have a better understanding of reporters and how they go about their jobs.

It is a subjective work. I have been a reporter for sixty years. I spent more than four decades at CBS News and more than a decade before that as a newspaperman and in other jobs in journalism. I can hardly be totally objective about a profession that I have loved since I got my first job at the age of twenty. This was my fourteenth campaign, and I believe I learned enough in those years to ask the right questions. Over the last two years I have talked to voters from California to Florida, and with my colleague Lucy Boyd, I traveled from New Hampshire to South Carolina and then to both party nominating conventions and the presidential and vice presidential debates. We talked to candidates, politicians, and pollsters, and most of all working reporters. In mid-2016, my friend Andrew Schwartz, the chief of communications at the Center for Strategic & International Studies (CSIS) and I began a series of forty-two podcasts with reporters and executives from across the communications landscape. It was a learning experience for us. Our hope is that it will prove useful to both those who create journalism and those who consume it.

We have no intention of "shutting up," as Trump advisor Bannon suggests, nor did we encounter any journalist along the way who felt so inclined.

Rather than silence, our hope is this book will cause more conversation about how we can better do our job of keeping Americans informed. We believe that is important.

—Bob Schieffer

───────────○───────────

Part One

HOW WE GOT FROM THERE TO HERE

How we get the news is always in a state of change. In America, it was a fairly orderly process when there were three television networks and a newspaper in every town. But cable eroded the network hold on audience, and the digital age plunged newspapers into an economic crisis and produced so much news it was difficult if not impossible to process. It all came to a head during the most unusual political campaign in modern history.

Chapter 1

———————O———————

Are We Getting
the Right Stuff?

THE 2016 ELECTION was unlike anything in American history—a contest between two candidates that most voters neither liked nor trusted but it produced more than an improbable winner.

It also revealed just how divided the nation was over issues ranging from the economy to law and order and race. Not since the O. J. Simpson trial when polls showed a majority of white people thought Simpson guilty and most African Americans believed he was innocent have the differences in opinion been so varied among blacks and whites, men and women, rich and poor, young and old.

It laid bare as well the weakness of the electoral process itself, which has become so odious that more and more officeholders and qualified, would-be candidates want nothing to do with it. They find the unending demand to raise money onerous, the travel exhausting, and the gridlock that prevents them from accomplishing anything simply more than they can endure.

When I was a child my grandmother thought I would grow up to be president of the United States because that's what every grandmother wished for her grandchild, but as the election of 2016 unfolded, I heard few parents or grandparents say, "I hope my child grows up to be a politician." Such is the disdain in which many Americans now hold the political class and those around it.

Perhaps that was part of the reason Americans of all political persuasions found it difficult to believe or trust anything said by candidates, their surrogates, or even the media.

Perhaps as well, that is at least part of the answer to the question I was asked most often in 2016: Why did the choice come down to those two? The sad but obvious truth is that too many times, the best of us want nothing to do with politics or holding public office.

The election also brought to the fore what many within the profession have been trying to deal with for years: journalism has been turned upside down by a technology revolution, newspapers are at a crisis point, and the state of the media may well have affected the election.

More than a hundred and twenty-six daily newspapers have shut down over the last decade, and the majority of those that have managed to survive have made drastic cuts in editorial staff. Many no longer have staff sufficient to cover traditional beats on a full-time basis, let alone send reporters to cover their state legislatures or their local members of congress in Washington. A recent study by the Pew Foundation showed that twenty-one of the fifty states do not have a single daily newspaper with a Washington-based reporter who covers the state delegation in Congress. Investigative reporting has become to many local papers a fond memory, something they simply no longer have the manpower to even contemplate.

By 2004, one reporter in eight lived in New York, Washington, or Los Angeles, but by 2014 that number was down to one in five, according to a study by *Washington Post*.

In many parts of the country outside those metropolitan areas, it's no longer a question of whether readers are getting biased news, it's whether they are getting any news—or at least reliable news.

As the author of the *Post* study Jim Tankersley wrote: "When the corner grocery in Michigan is driven out of business by a big chain based in Arkansas, the people in Michigan still have somewhere to shop. If regional news outlets die who will dig up corruption by their local lawmakers?"

So where do Americans get their news today? Are we getting the news we need to make intelligent decisions as good citizens? That is what we set out to investigate in this study.

Americans have access to more information than any humans who have inhabited Earth at any time in history. But are we more informed, or simply overwhelmed by so much information that we are unable to process it?

These questions grew out of a discussion in early 2015 with John Hamre, who heads the Center for Strategic & International Studies. Hamre, his communications chief—Andrew Schwartz—and I were talking politics over coffee. But as is often the case with Washington conversations, we had no idea what was about to unfold.

What we did recognize was that the coming campaign promised to be different. The threat of terrorism and an endless series of violent episodes had left the electorate in an uneasy, sour mood. The partisan divide had grown wider as Washington gridlock had grown tighter. As Washington dithered and dawdled, many found it difficult to believe politicians or journalists. The number of Americans who identified as Republicans or Democrats was near an all-time low. And all this was playing out as technology was changing the way our campaigns were being conducted and how we were getting the news about them.

As newspapers across the country were devoting less coverage to politics, social media was playing a more and more important role in people's lives.

Even in places where newspapers were still publishing, print was literally the last place younger Americans looked for news. As the curtain was rising on a campaign to select the next president of the United States, there was so much information bombarding us from all sides it was difficult to sort out what mattered from what didn't, and much of it was wrong. Not just wrong, but dead wrong on purpose.

Hamre was clearly concerned. A defense intellectual who served as deputy secretary of defense in the Clinton administration, Hamre is widely respected by Democrats and Republicans. In his long career in and out of government, he has never been one to make snap judgments, but that day he said, "The state of journalism is a national security issue, if our people don't have a clear understanding what our problems are and the threats we face, they can't come together on solutions to fix them."

"That has to be one of the reasons for our growing inability to find consensus and that's what this campaign should be all about."

We would soon learn that was *not* what Campaign 2016 was about, and it would have the opposite effect: it did not show a path to national unity but left the country more divided.

From the invention of the printing press to radio and television, satellites and now digital, the one constant in communication has always been constant change—the change brought by advances in technology. Hamre's remark reminded me of a conversation, decades earlier, with the now deceased *New York Times* reporter Jim Naughton. We had covered the Gerald Ford White House together, and he had gone on to head the Poynter Institute, a journalism think tank. On that long ago day, we were talking about the change that everyone in journalism was talking about then—the changes brought on by the recent rise of cable television and the coming of Fox News, talk radio, and other opinion-based radio and cable outlets.

In those years we were emerging from the "gatekeeper era" when most people got their news from one of the three networks or from the local newspaper in their town or city.

"We're no longer basing our opinions on the same data," Naughton said. "It used to be that we got our facts from the front pages of our local newspapers or the wire services or the networks.

"Maybe we agreed or disagreed with their editorials or opinion pieces, but we accepted what was on the front pages or what Walter Cronkite reported as true and we based our own opinions on that.

"Now," he said, "we're no longer basing our opinions on the same stuff—some folks get one set of facts from one outlet and other folks get another set of facts from another outlet, no wonder they come to different conclusions."

Naughton's prescient observation about the changing face of journalism has only intensified in the age of digital streaming and social media. Americans still go to the source they feel most comfortable with to get their news—but not always for the same reasons.

Bill Brock, the former Tennessee senator and one-time head of the Republican Party said recently that many Americans choose their favorite channel (or website) not to get just the latest information but "to get the ammo to back up their previously formed opinions." And it was getting harder to separate opinion from fact. That task has become even more difficult with the proliferation of so-called fake news, news made up out of whole cloth: "we never really went to the moon," "the Sandy Hook shooting and 9/11 were staged by the government or other sinister forces," "President Obama was not born in the United States," and even more bizarre tales that now fill the Internet.

Rumor and innuendo have always been a part of most cultures, but what has changed is universal access to the web and the ability to transmit information, true or false, to literally billions of people in milliseconds.

When I came into journalism in the 1950s, there was a debate about whether journalists should be licensed, as is the case with other professionals such as doctors and lawyers. Of course not, we said, our license is the First Amendment. If you have a barrel of ink and a printing press, you're a publisher and you can say or print anything that's on your mind as long as it's true.

Today it's no longer so simple.

Technology has eliminated the need for ink and a printing press. All we need now is a computer (meaning phone) and that phone gives us access to worldwide circulation instantly. The impact of that has been staggering. It has changed more than our journalism. It has changed our politics and culture, redefined our definition of privacy, coarsened our language, and shortened our attention span and patience. When the Sunday *New York Times Magazine* devoted an entire issue to the Middle East, the editor felt compelled to ask readers to be patient and in so many words assured them that the long article was worth the read.

Those who despair at the low level to which campaign rhetoric sank during the 2016 campaign need look no further for a template than the threads that follow blog posts that generally devolve from the inane to the profane. "You're a jerk!" "No, you're a bigger jerk!" "Well. You're a blank, blank jerk!" And on and on, because that's how we talk. Arguably, one reason that Donald Trump was able to connect with his core supporters was that he spoke as so many people write in their Internet posts. Apparently, they found his style familiar and comfortable.

I have often argued that the most successful politicians are those who have mastered the dominant communication medium of their time. The Founders were gifted writers in an era when most people got their news in written form. Franklin Roosevelt was the first politician to recognize the best way to communicate by radio (his fireside chats were delivered as if he were speaking to a family gathered around the kitchen table, which many were). John Kennedy was the first to master live television. Will we look back on the 2016 election and conclude that Trump was the first to understand the power of Twitter?

The impact of the new technology on journalism has been no less profound than the other changes wrought by the web. Whether it's a teenager musing at midnight about the meaning of life on his blog, a local newspaper publisher trying to find new sources of revenue to replace the money lost when want ads found a new home on eBay, or even the mighty *New York Times* that embarked in 2016 on a project to produce videos for Facebook's newsfeed, journalists find themselves in a new world. Even the *Times*'s own public editor wondered if the newspaper was going too far, too fast. But the reason the *Times* turned out a Facebook-ready product was not hard to fathom. The *Times* too, has bills to pay, and Facebook reaches 1.5 billion people. There are worse ways to introduce prospective readers to the *Times*.

The *Times* is not the only organization making major changes. The *Washington Post*—one of the rare newspaper success stories since its purchase by billionaire Jeff Bezos—no longer sees its first priority as getting out the morning newspaper. The priority now is the website. When a story has been edited and put through the same vetting process as before, it goes on the web. Scoops are no longer held for the print version.

"We not only adapted to the digital environment but embraced the digital environment," *Post* executive editor Martin Baron told us.

Baron felt he had no choice, but the decision has paid off spectacularly. In 2016 sometimes more than one hundred million people in a single month saw the *Post*'s digital report.

"We live in a mobile society," he said. "Everybody expects that they should be able to get any news at any time wherever they are on a device that fits into a pocket. They can get that kind of information on a smartphone. It's projected that within four years, something like 80 percent of the world's population will have access to a smartphone. That's amazing. The world is changing and we have to change with it."

Like the big newspapers, the major broadcasters are also retooling.

David Rhodes, the forty-two-year-old wunderkind president of CBS News, says the first thing that journalists and news organizations must recognize is the obvious: it is a different world. To compete in that world, Rhodes introduced a new streaming service, CBSN, a twenty-four-hour digital news service that can be received only on phones and computers or through various digital transmission services such as Roku.

"People know about developments much faster, and they want the news now," he told us. "That changes the whole competitive landscape. It used to be you had a lot of people employed going out trying to learn information and get pictures. Now you need a similar number of people to sift through the overwhelmingly available information and pictures just to decide what is true and what is not."

CBS News more or less invented radio news during the Murrow-led years of World War II. When it expanded its Evening News from fifteen to thirty minutes in 1963 during the Cronkite era, it set the pattern under which network news still operates. Change has not always come easily to the organization. During the earliest days of television, Ed Murrow and his radio stars resisted appearing on the new television medium. They feared the pictures would distract from their words. So it was not Murrow but a little-known reporter named Douglas Edwards who became the first anchor of the CBS Evening News, a post he held for seven years until Walter Cronkite replaced him in 1962.

For decades, the Evening News was CBS News' premier broadcast, and the producer, Don Hewitt, who later created 60 Minutes, was never afraid to think out of the box. In an effort to relieve Edwards from having to look down at the script, he tried at one point to have him learn Braille, believing he could touch the script with his fingers while looking directly at the camera. It brought new meaning to hand-eye coordination, but somehow it never worked out. The format, however—a headquarters-based anchor who throws it to a reporter on the scene—survives today. (Teleprompters solved the eye-contact problem.)

Nevertheless, as technology changed, CBS and the other network news organizations changed with it, and just as priorities have shifted at the *Washington Post* and the *New York Times*, they have shifted as well at CBS News.

No longer is the Evening News the only fiefdom in the CBS kingdom that executives worry about. Big scoops that were once held for the Evening News now appear with regularity on *CBS This Morning*, and before that, they may have aired on CBSN, the twenty-four-hour digital platform. And chances are the correspondent who reported the story may have already tweeted the story's headline.

CBS News is no longer just a broadcaster but a media company that operates on a variety of platforms. Its website provides what amounts to a digital wire service similar to the Associated Press. CBSN, which CBS launched in 2014, has the look and feel of an all-news cable service but also features an archive that provides important speeches and events on demand. It delivered gavel-to-gavel coverage from both the 2016 Democratic and Republican conventions, at times drawing audiences larger than the network broadcasts.

While big companies like CBS and the *Washington Post* are building audience through the new technology, it is local newspapers that have been hardest hit. While 126 newspapers have closed since 2004, others have drastically scaled back editorial staff, and with the reductions, reduced coverage. Print circulation dropped another 7 percent last year, in line with the drop of 25 percent since 1990.

As newspapers have closed, retrenched, and reorganized, digital media outlets have sprung up like mushrooms after an overnight rain. Some such as Politico, which was founded by two veteran *Washington Post* political reporters, John Harris and Jim VandeHei, have had remarkable success and have proven to be reliable sources for news. Still others have proven to be little more than propaganda sources that generate volumes of information that is often wrong by design—what we have come to know as "fake news."

It was in the spring of 2015 that Andrew Schwartz and I with the help of Lucy Boyd, who joined CBS News as a political researcher after obtaining her master's degree from the Kennedy School at Harvard, set out to explore this new communications industry in an effort to understand how well it is serving the American people. Are we—as John Hamre wondered—more or less informed than we once were? To find out, we began the old-fashioned way: talking to people at all levels and from every part of this ever-changing news-gathering landscape. By mid-2016 many of our conversations became weekly podcasts distributed by iTunes. All of these conversations in written and oral form can be found on the CSIS website.

Our hope is that this book can be a guide to the new world of journalism, the good and the bad along with examples of the innovation and changes that today's journalists are making to meet the challenges of this unfolding era.

We found it to be an amazing, often surprising story.

The way we communicate has and continues to change rapidly and dramatically, and it has affected every facet of American life.

And John Hamre was right. The state of journalism is a national security issue.

Chapter 2

---O---

The Challenge of Campaign 2016
How Do You Solve a Problem Like the Donald?

DONALD TRUMP WAS THE MOST UNUSUAL CANDIDATE I ever covered in the most unusual campaign I can remember in the most unusual year of the more than four decades I spent in Washington.

How unusual was it?

It was the year one candidate, Jeb Bush, raised $115 million, and it seemed to make no difference.

It was the year when the Democratic candidate Hillary Clinton was asked why she took more than $600,000 in speaking fees from Goldman Sachs and responded, "It's what they offered."

It was the year former Republican House Speaker John Boehner called Republican presidential candidate Ted Cruz "Lucifer in the flesh" and a devil worshiper's society objected.

It was the year Donald Trump called on the Russian Intelligence Service to delve into Clinton's emails.

It was the year a proud Socialist, Bernie Sanders, announced he "was not a capitalist" and nearly beat out Hillary Clinton for the Democratic Party nomination.

It was the year billionaire Trump flew around the country in his private jet bragging about things the rich never brag about—his wealth and how he had accumulated it by taking advantage of tax loopholes—all the while preaching that he was the friend of the working man.

I said I'd "never seen anything like it" so many times my younger colleagues started a game when off duty. When I popped up on television, they took a drink every time I used the phrase. Apparently designated drivers looked out for their safety.

It was hard to find anyone in or out of politics who had seen anything like it. Early on many reporters dismissed him as a joke, and there was little to argue against that. He broke every rule in politics. He insulted women, made fun of the disabled, called American hero John McCain a loser, came off as an apologist for Russian leader Vladimir Putin, and cast aspersions on Hispanics, the fastest-growing segment of the American population. A week before the Republican Convention I went to Capitol Hill and couldn't find a single Republican leader in the Senate who thought he was going to win. By the time of the Republican Convention, they were working to prevent a Democratic takeover of the Senate as well. So they were not surprised, nor was I, that he would approach Election Day behind in every poll. Nor were Trump's own people. I was told by a reliable source that Trump's own pollsters gave him only a 20 percent chance of winning, and yet he won on a simple promise: "make America great again." Trump's strategy seems obvious in retrospect. He figured out early on that if he offered himself to enough television programs, he would be invited to appear on some of them, and as we used to say "he was good copy." He said things people remembered—some true, some dubious—but his core supporters seemed to care little for details, or even truth. They just liked his brash style.

Television news programs, especially cable outlets, were criticized for giving him too much free airtime, but Trump just kept pounding away. Using his celebrity and sometimes making outrageous claims, one television appearance led to more. Often he would just call in by phone from his perch high above Manhattan in Trump Tower.

Surprisingly to some, the only Sunday show host who refused to let him call in by phone was Fox News moderator Chris Wallace. "I just decided no," Wallace said. "And I wound up getting one Sunday interview during the whole campaign compared to a half dozen or so for some of the other shows." (CBS *This Morning* also turned down phone interviews.) Some critics said he got no pushback from television hosts. In fact, he was often challenged, but he was getting so much exposure it overwhelmed the pushback. He would be challenged on one program, but as that was happening, he would top it with charges on another outlet.

Whether Trump knew it or not, his was a version of a political strategy first defined by Lynton Crosby, an Australian political consultant who later worked in the campaigns of British prime minister David Cameron. Crosby called it the "Dead Cat Strategy," which held that no matter what the conversation at a dinner party was about, if you threw a dead cat on the table people started talking about the dead cat.

Time and again, no matter what the campaign conversation was about, Trump threw another dead cat into the mix and people talked about that and him.

"Early on," said Dan Balz, the *Washington Post* reporter who has become the dean of political journalists, "Trump would get on television early in the morning either in person or by phone and say things that the other candidates would have to respond to through the day."

As the criticism grew over the amount of airtime Trump was getting, I asked Mika Brzezinski and Joe Scarborough, the hosts of MSNBC's *Morning Joe*, why they never gave Hillary Clinton equal time.

"Getting an interview with her is like getting an interview with Mother Teresa," Brzezinski told me.

That in a sentence summed up the difference in the Clinton and Trump campaigns.

Whatever else can be said about it, the Clinton campaign was operating the old way and by the old rules—a huge, consultant-heavy staff focused on raising money and dependent on constant polling to develop policy statements and talking points in an effort to "control the narrative." By the old rules, campaigns shielded candidates from situations in which they might get unexpected questions or tough follow-ups. Clinton did few interviews, and campaign workers seemed more determined to shield her from voters and reporters than finding ways to connect with them.

One picture that summed up the approach appeared early in the campaign during a Midwestern parade. As Clinton marched,

she was surrounded by aides carrying ropes that prevented bystand-
ers from getting close enough to touch her and reporters from getting close enough to ask her questions. The walking rope corral got
more attention that day than anything she said.

When she did do interviews they were so laden with talking
points they seemed rehearsed and stale. That made a stark contrast
to Trump's nonstop rambling about anything and everything.

With Trump, you never knew what he was going to say. With
Clinton the statements were often so familiar you could almost say
them along with her.

"He just understood the modern era better than the other politicians," Balz told me. "He was a professional television performer."

As I wandered through a Trump rally with colleague Lucy Boyd
during the South Carolina primary, supporter after supporter told
us, "I just admire him for speaking out."

The Trump campaign became a campaign in which attitude
counted more than issues. When Trump made claims that he
would build a wall along the Texas border to keep Mexicans out,
many supporters I talked to before and after the election told me
they didn't take him literally.

"I never believed he would build that wall," a Trump supporter
told me the day after the election. "But I knew he was concerned
about immigration and that he would do something about it. The
rest of them just talked in circles."

Maureen Dowd, the Pulitzer Prize–winning columnist for the
New York Times, has covered Trump for years. This was her sev-
enth presidential campaign, but this one was different. As it was
moving into its final months, I asked her to compare it with previous campaigns.

"I usually think of campaigns as Shakespearian because I stud-
ied Shakespeare in college, but this one was more like that old
movie, *Who Killed Jessica Rabbit*, which was Toons (animated car-
toon characters) interacting with humans.

"Trump is a 'toon running against a human,' and the collision of
those two cultures makes it very hard for the press to know how to
deal with him.

"It's a whole new thing. The collision of reality television and
social media with politics. Trump is the Kim Kardashian of politics.

He is dominating every news cycle, stepping on his own news cycle, then tweeting something that ruins the message.

"And it's funny that it's a seventy-year-old man who's introduced Twitter to the campaign so it's a whole new kettle of fish!"

Joe Scarborough told me one of the great challenges with Trump was that "he is unmoored ideologically. He's unmoored to any worldview. He's unmoored to objective facts. So it's a constantly moving target."

After Trump attacked the Muslim Gold Star family who spoke at the Democratic Convention, I began to wonder if he had decided he didn't want to be president and was looking for a way to lose.

Maureen Dowd believes he was—some of the time. "I think sometimes he's probably scared. But then he sees the Secret Service in front of Trump Tower and he's thrilled," she said.

Whatever his doubts, if he was looking for a way to lose, the ploy proved spectacularly unsuccessful.

That the election left the country angry and divided should not be surprising after a contest between two candidates that a majority neither liked nor trusted.

Both candidates blamed the press when things didn't go their way, which is not unusual, and there will be endless commentary about how the press—newspaper and television—covered the campaign: Was Trump given too much free time on television? Was there too little focus on issues? Too much emphasis on polling and the horse race? Too much negativity?

Much of the criticism was justified: too much misinformation made its way into the national conversation. In an effort to show balance, too many so-called strategists and surrogates were given far more credibility than they deserved, and too many times news organizations credited one candidate or another with narrow leads when in fact, their leads fell within the margins of error. Still, it seems fair to point out that it was a campaign less about issues than attitude. One Trump surrogate went so far as to say, "facts don't really matter anymore," and the Oxford Dictionary's word of the year was *post-truth*.

Reporters can fact check (there was more of it than ever in 2016), and we can keep watch on campaigns in the same way we keep an eye on government and how tax dollars are spent. But we don't run campaigns, nor should we, any more than we should run the government. Candidates run the campaigns. We are there to report what they say or do and point out when and how that doesn't jibe with the facts. There was little positive campaign reporting because there was little positive to report about. When candidates fill debates with arguments about the size of body parts, there's little to feel good about or cheer. It was a disgrace and we said that.

We pointed out many times that the candidates weren't talking about issues, and when they proposed unrealistic solutions as Trump did when he talked about expelling eleven million undocumented immigrants, we said so. Nor was there any shortage of attention to the Clinton emails.

I found plenty of people who liked or disliked Hillary Clinton and Donald Trump, but I didn't find anyone who thought they needed more information about either to cast their vote.

Where the press erred, as one reporter put it, was in taking what Trump said literally but not seriously while his core supporters took him seriously but never literally. That raises a question for future coverage: When we quote a candidate should we add "but I don't think he really means it"? I vote no on that one.

Trump won because too many people in the battleground states felt they were being left behind. That seemed especially true in rural areas, where 15 percent of Americans still live, a segment of the population larger than the much-sought-after Hispanic vote. They were worried about jobs, about their future, and their safety, and so they took a flyer on Trump whether or not they really believed him.

Clinton, for all the money she raised and the enormous campaign team and consultants she put together, was never able to craft a message that got through to those people who had once been the heart and soul of the Democratic Party. As Trump kept talking, Clinton was never able to generate much excitement beyond the fund-raisers she arranged among the elites of Hollywood and New York.

The Clinton team felt that the FBI public disclosure that it was reopening the email investigation in the closing days of the campaign tipped the election to Trump. In fact, late deciders in Florida, Pennsylvania, Michigan, and Wisconsin did go for Trump by big margins, and the disclosure may well have been a factor. But there was another question never sufficiently answered: Why did Clinton choose to open a private email account in the first place? Why did no one warn her that such a practice risked more trouble than it was worth?

Or maybe it was not all that complicated. Maybe, as former First Lady Barbara Bush suggested early in 2014, maybe people were just tired of Kennedys, Clintons, and Bushes.

"This is a great country . . . and if we can't find more than three families to run for high office, that's silly," she said.

Silly or not, when the process coughs up two candidates that most voters didn't like, we should not have been surprised that the result was arguably the worst campaign of modern times.

Chapter 3

─────────○─────────

The Numbers Guys
What the Pollsters Missed

IF ANYONE SHOULD KNOW, Peter Hart should know. He is the dean of American pollsters, so I put the question to him: pollsters took a real beating in 2016; was the criticism justified?

"Sure," he said. "Because if you look at most people who talked about this election, they told you that Hillary Clinton would win."

Hart says national polls were not that far off. Both his poll, the Wall Street Journal/NBC News survey, and the CBS News'/New York Times poll, showed Clinton winning the popular vote by about four points, and she won by two.

"But in terms of state polls, there were a lot of wide mistakes," he said. "Essentially, we don't have anybody overseeing the polling industry. Some of (the state polls) are quite good and they've had a long reputation; others just showed up. And we don't make any differentiation between good and bad polls."

This was further complicated, he says, by reliance on the trend by some websites to publish "averages" of the various polls.

"If you are a wine drinker," he asks, "would you take a dollar bottle of wine and put it in with a $300 bottle and say, let's see how the average of the wine is? Why is it any better to take a zillion polls, some good, some bad, and put it altogether?"

My personal criticism of how the polls were used was that too many times we downplayed or failed to mention entirely the margins of error.

Television reporters would say "the poll shows candidate so and so leading by one point" when in fact there is no such thing as a one-point lead. If a poll's margin of error is plus or minus four points, for example, the candidate with the "one-point lead" may be leading by five points or losing by three. What the poll is reflecting is that the race is very close, too close to call.

While Hart agrees with that, his criticism is more nuanced. He believes he made three basic mistakes.

He knew from the beginning that people did not trust Clinton, and he underestimated how much integrity counted in the election.

Pollsters structured their polls to reflect feelings in the East, West, Midwest, and South and did not put enough emphasis on the Rust Belt, which proved crucial. "After it was over," he said, "we went back and looked at it and Trump was winning there. We didn't pick it up" (nor did the Clinton campaign, which stopped polling in individual states in October).

Some 18 to 20 percent of voters had negative feelings about Trump and Clinton. Early on the two candidates were getting equal shares of that vote. Only at the end did Trump begin to move up in that category, and on Election Day he got 47 percent of that vote to 30 percent for Clinton.

Was all that another way of saying Hillary Clinton lost it rather than Donald Trump won it?

In Hart's opinion, the answer to that question is yes, because he believes she never corrected her basic problem—that people simply did not trust her.

"We knew that from the absolute beginning," he said. "We measured it in 2007 before she ran against Barack Obama, we measured it in 2015 and 2016.

"Essentially she lost because she never corrected her deficiencies. Instead of being unpacked, they got packed on whether it was the speeches on Wall Street or the emails or the Comey report, all those things kept reinforcing one thing: you can't trust Hillary Clinton."

Hart has run the NBC/Wall Street Journal poll since 1989, and over the years he has polled for numerous institutions as well as fifty-five senators and forty governors, so when he offers political advice (which he seldom does publicly), it is worth noting.

He says the Clinton campaign never heard the voter. They could have dealt with the integrity issue, and in his opinion, they could have made her more sympathetic.

"If I'd been in charge of Hillary Clinton's campaign I would have demonstrated who I'm fighting for and who I'm fighting against," he said. "When EpiPen suddenly raised the price of life-saving drugs, I would have put her out in front of that headquarters and said these people are going to be held accountable or we are going to change things. And when the Wells Fargo scandal came out with their problems, I would have put her right in front of one of their banks and said these banks are going to pay a price and they are going to either behave in an ethical fashion or we are going to take them to a court and finish them. She gave (voters) six points or four-point programs, but she never connected with them."

But if voters didn't vote for Hillary because they didn't trust her, why did they vote for Trump? After all, they didn't trust him either.

Hart's response: "At the end of the day, what happened essentially is that voters said, 'You know something? He's repulsive, I don't like it but I like what he wants to do.'"

How was he able to get away with the things he said—insulting war hero John McCain, belittling a handicapped reporter, berating a Gold Star family, making misogynistic comments toward Megyn Kelly, and the infamous "grab 'em by the p____" sex tape?

"The rise of incivility," Hart said. "We're pretending as though somehow Donald Trump was exempt from that. No, it all started going back to Jerry Springer twenty-five years ago. Look at some of the things on the Internet . . . we have become inured to so many of the things that are out there."

To put it another way, Donald Trump was not having an impact on the culture but simply reflecting a culture that has grown more impolite and vulgar.

"We thought Donald Trump was something unusual," Hart continued. "All he is, is part of the 'amateur professionals'—that's Airbnb, it's Uber, it's all the things that are happening.

"We thought the establishment was the thing. No. Bush was through. Clinton was through. It was not about money. It was about SpaceX, Elon Musk, Amazon. All these things that are changing our lives and they are all connected."

The election has left the country deeply divided, but for all the advances in technology, Hart says sampling public opinion is becoming harder, not easier. The coming of the mobile telephone has turned polling upside down. When most voters had landlines, you could call representative samples in the various area codes and know who you were calling. No more. Most young people and those in lower economic classes no longer have landlines.

That and telemarketing has led to the most serious polling problem, "respondent unwillingness."

"Before, it used to be a privilege to be interviewed. Now it's a bother," he said. "We get under 10 percent of respondents willing to take a poll. Well, how about the 91 percent who are unwilling that we are leaving out? To underline that, CBS News pollsters used to call 3,000 people in order to get 1,500 people for a national poll. Today, they must contact 30,000 to get 1,500."

Still, Hart believes the bigger issue is we've stopped listening to the voices of voters and we've started thinking in statistics or dynamics and analytics, and he says that just doesn't work. As he put it, "Analytics tell you one thing but they don't tell you what's in people's hearts."

That suggests more focus groups, and for journalists more of what the old political reporters used to do—knock on doors and talk to more people on the street.

As pollsters look for new and better methodology, Hart doesn't need new tools to understand one thing: the election outcome reflected the country's deep division.

"Essentially, we're unhappy with where we are as a country," he told me. "We were unhappy with the people in power, the status quo.

"It was a change election."

Chapter 4

————————————O————————————

And That's the Way
It Is, er, Was*
Newspapers, Gatekeepers, and a More Orderly Time

WHEN JILL ABRAMSON WAS RUNNING the *New York Times*, she used to talk about the great pleasure of reading a newspaper.

In 2011, Abramson became the first woman to be named executive editor of the *Times*, and like so many of her generation both inside and outside journalism, her morning began reading the newspaper.

"What I always enjoyed most about reading the paper," she once told me, "was not just finding the stories I was interested in but turning through the pages and discovering stories about things I might not have thought about.

"We often go to the web to look up something. That's not necessarily the reason we pick up a newspaper."

As pleasurable as reading a newspaper may be, it is a pleasure fewer and fewer Americans have chosen to enjoy. And the younger they are, the less likely they are to depend on newspapers.

News habits are slow to change. Like Abramson, until the Kennedy assassination in 1963, most Americans got their news from newspapers, a habit that had begun in the mid-nineteenth century.

———————————

*Walter Cronkite always ended his broadcast, "and that's the way it is."

25

Newspapers had been fairly dull reading in those days, but two enterprising publishers, Joseph Pulitzer and William Randolph Hearst, had changed that. Using the newly invented telegraph, they printed news from afar within hours after it happened. More importantly, Pulitzer biographer James M. Morris told me they recognized that people liked to read about themselves and their own neighborhood.

"Pulitzer figured out that the O'Shaunasseys who lived on the lower East Side of Manhattan cared more about what was happening there than who was going to what society ball, so he told his reporters to forget the parties and write about the lower East Side, and circulation soared," Morris said.

Hearst was doing the same thing, and both men began selling advertising, which made their papers financially independent from the political parties. Fierce competition led to outrageous sensationalism by both men, but the pattern for news habits was set. People turned to their local newspapers to find out what was happening near them and abroad. News consumers have always favored local news over foreign news. There is an old saying in journalism, "When two stories are of equal importance, lead with the one that's closest to the City Hall flag pole." With the outbreak of World War II, foreign news became local news. Radio news pioneered by Ed Murrow and his "boys" came into its own as Americans gathered around their radios for late developments. Every American family had a relative or a friend or an acquaintance involved. American lives changed overnight with rationing and shortages. Women joined the workforce by the thousands as men went off to fight the war. The war was the biggest news in every American town and city. Big-city newspapers sent reporters to cover the war. The dailies became the trusted sources of record for not just local news but war news as well.

All that changed with the death of President Kennedy in Dallas on that fateful morning of November 22, 1963. For the first time the entire nation focused on one event, and people were seeing it in real time, on television. From that day until this, more Americans would get their news from television than any other source.

Americans were so accustomed to getting their news in print that an unusual phenomenon became evident in the hours after the shooting. Even though they had just seen the shooting on television, many sought printed confirmation. Thirty miles from Dallas at the *Fort Worth Star-Telegram* where I worked in those days, people lined up around the block where the newspaper was located and waited to buy the newspaper "extras," which we kept churning out through the afternoon. It was as if those who left their televisions to buy newspapers couldn't believe what they had just seen on their television screens—it wasn't somehow valid—until they saw it written down on a printed page.

Years later after I had joined CBS News, I realized television had become the validating medium. I noticed that delegates at a political convention were crowding around my television monitor to see how an event they were seeing with their own eyes in person looked on TV. For that group it was as if the event wasn't really "official" until they had seen it on television.

On that awful Dallas weekend, Americans also learned how news is gathered. Until that day, they were accustomed to getting their news from journalism's finished product, the carefully edited story that appeared in their newspaper, or in those early television days, an edited piece on film.

That weekend, they saw not just the horrible news but journalists at work gathering the information that made their stories, and it was not always an orderly process—reporters shouting and pushing to get information. The pictures shocked many viewers and raised questions in their minds about reporters' credibility.

Even as a majority of Americans turned to television for news, newspapers continued to exert enormous influence in their areas of circulation. Local television stations might have more viewers than newspapers had readers, but with smaller staffs the TV stations often depended on the newspapers to do the basic coverage and sometimes simply rewrote newspaper stories, then broadcast them on their newscasts.

During the Vietnam War, such was the power of the *New York Times* that network correspondents in Vietnam would sometimes tip *Times* correspondents if they had a good story. (In those days it usually took three days for film stories shipped from Saigon to get to New York.) The correspondents knew that if the story they had packaged on film showed up on the *Times* front page the day their film arrived, it increased the chances of their story appearing on television that evening. As CBS and then NBC extended their evening news broadcasts to a half hour in 1963, their power and influence expanded. Walter Cronkite on CBS and the NBC duo of Chet Huntley and David Brinkley attained a celebrity equal to Hollywood stars. Washington beat reporters such as CBS News White House correspondent Dan Rather, Capitol Hill correspondent Roger Mudd, and State Department correspondent Marvin Kalb became more well known than many of the politicians they covered.

It was a Golden Age for television news. The largest audiences of news consumers in American history gathered around their televisions for the evening news broadcasts. Walter Cronkite became "the most trusted man in America." Brinkley became the first television anchor who spoke in the conversational way most people speak, and he was loved for his wry humor and irony. The evening newscasts became a national habit, a common experience that almost everyone shared. It should also be said that much of television's early influence and huge ratings came because the network news had no competition, as Texas A&M professor Johanna Dunaway noted during a recent study. During the dinner hour, she reported, the networks presented only news broadcasts. With the coming of cable and more independent stations, viewers had other choices, and when given a choice, viewers nearly always chose entertainment and the size of news audiences began to shrink.

Ted Turner's cable outlet CNN introduced an all-news format in 1980 but had so little impact in the beginning that many in the industry referred to it dismissively as the Chicken Noodle Network. That changed on the first night of the Gulf War in 1991 when the networks found themselves badly scooped. When the coalition bombing campaign began, CNN was the only news outlet technically able to broadcast from inside Iraq. CNN's Peter Arnett, John Holliman, and Bernard Shaw broadcast gripping reports from their Baghdad hotel room as bombs fell around them. The Chicken Noodle Network had broken the mold for television reporting, and TV news would never be the same.

As competition for viewer attention increased overall, audiences grew, but audiences for individual news organizations would never again be as large as they had been in the early 1960s and into the 1970s. With the coming of the web and then digital outlets, choices to find news and entertainment multiplied a hundredfold. Again audiences for individual outlets dwindled as overall audiences continued to grow.

Television remains the place where most Americans (57 percent) still get news, but the Pew Foundation reports there is a significant generational divide. The vast majority of those who depend on television are over thirty. Only 27 percent of those under thirty choose television.

Amy Mitchell, who monitors media for Pew, told us in the summer of 2016 the shift away from print has been even more dramatic.

As the 2016 campaign was beginning, Pew asked people where they were turning for election news. Only 5 percent said they had learned something about the campaign during the previous week from a paper newspaper. More people had learned something from TV, radio, websites, or cable—all other sources of news—than from a newspaper.

Pew's reporting showed that younger adults were more likely to name social media as their main source of news. Pew reported fully 62 percent of American adults now get some news on social media.

News organizations were blindsided by the rise of social media. Not surprising. Technology always runs ahead of our ability to understand, exploit, or control it. How many soldiers died before generals understood you don't attack a machine gun nest by marching directly into the machine gun's line of fire?

So it was with the web. No one died during the shifts toward social media, but the communications landscape is littered with failing news organizations.

At first publishers ignored the web. Then in an early effort to compete, they created websites where they gave away the news product they had financed with paid advertising. That immediately backfired. News consumers came to believe the news was free, a commodity to which they were entitled. The music industry was dealing with the same attitude with no less success.

Over the last decade, newspapers have found themselves in a desperate fight for survival. Pew began 2016's annual State of the

News Media report with this sentence: "Eight years after the Great Recession sent the U.S. newspaper industry into a tailspin, the pressures facing America's newsrooms have intensified to nothing less than a reorganization of the industry itself, one that impacts the experiences of even those news consumers unaware of the tectonic shifts taking place."

In fact, Pew's researchers concluded 2015 had been the single worst year since 2008. Circulation had fallen another 7 percent in one year, and with it came another drop in ad revenue of 8 percent. Shrinking budgets meant shrinking newsrooms. Newsroom jobs across the country stood at twenty-two thousand, only 39 percent of what they once were. Newspaper reporters accounted for less than a third of the journalists in Washington and only 38 percent of those covering state houses. Niche reporters for newsletters and similar outlets outnumbered both groups.

For newspapers, the future looks no better. Of the 126 newspapers that have closed over the past decade, two closed in the spring of 2016, including the 150-year-old *Oakland Tribune*, which has been melded into a combination of five other Back Bay area papers in California, including the *San Jose Mercury News*. On Fridays the new paper includes an insert for the people of Oakland with news about their city.

Historically, as technology has improved the speed and ease with which we distribute information, the power and influence of the news distributor has grown. More significantly, as people have become more informed, social change has followed—usually for the better.

The invention of the printing press not only relieved the writer's cramp that cursed the medieval monks who spent their lives copying the documents on which the history of western culture was recorded. More importantly, it made those documents available to a much wider audience. Literacy spread, and among other things, the ability to print information played a major role in the Protestant Reformation. Less significantly, it gave journalism its name. Printers pressed ink-covered letters onto paper, hence the term *the press* came to be.

Historical precedent aside, out-of-work reporters, editors, and publishers might be excused for failing to see the immediate benefit to society and public understanding that has come with the decline of newspapers brought on by technological advances.

Nor is there any evidence to suggest that the shift from print has made us more informed.

Even politicians who generally find ways to blame the press for most of their misfortune bemoan the lack of newspaper coverage at the local level. During the 2010 governor's race in Texas, a candidate who was flying around the state to announce his candidacy told me about arriving in a South Texas town's airport. A television cameraman greeted him and apologized that the station was unable to send a reporter "because we only have a reporter on Tuesday." The local newspaper sent no one.

"That makes it kind of hard to let people know why you're running," the candidate said.

While local newspapers have suffered the severest cutbacks, big papers such as the *Los Angeles Times* and *Chicago Tribune* have also been hit hard. In 2016, even the *Wall Street Journal*, owned by the highly successful media baron Rupert Murdoch and one of the most influential of the major newspapers, announced plans for significant staff cutbacks.

The reduction in news staffs has brought with it a decline in beat reporters—the traditional foundation on which news organizations large and small operate. One reporter covers city government, one hangs out at the police station, another covers education or important local industries. Good beat reporters come to reflect the culture of the beat they cover, and in my police beat days at the *Fort Worth Star-Telegram*, I always wore a snap-brim hat so I would look like a detective. Our agriculture reporter was named Calvin Pigg, but our editor insisted that was just a coincidence, as was the fact that a reporter named Monk Vance succeeded him.

Beat reporters must always guard against becoming too close to their sources, but because they are on the beat every day they develop an understanding of the institution they are covering, not just the stories that happen there. With cutbacks, many papers now send reporters to cover weekly city council meetings. They no longer go to city hall every day.

Washington Post editor Martin Baron understands the economic circumstances that brought the changes to papers smaller than his but says fewer reporters on the beats change the whole dynamic of news coverage from the state house to city hall and even lesser local government entities.

"Only one or two people to cover the governor, both houses of the legislature, every agency, policy and politics—it is not possible to do deep investigative reporting, and politicians know that which can lead to action that is not in the public interest," he said.

As Amy Mitchell has conducted her news surveys for Pew, she found evidence that politicians act differently when reporters are not there. She quoted one local politician who admitted that he "put things in different language" when reporters were present.

John Cutter, managing editor of the *Orlando Sentinel*, winner of three Pulitzers and one of the best local papers, says he feels the impact every day.

"We know there are things going on at some of the government meetings we used to staff with reporters," he told us. "The officials know it and we know it. Sometimes, it causes them to be less forthcoming in handing over routine documents that they know and we know we're entitled to. These days they are more apt to say 'sue us' if you want the information.

"One thing we depend on now are citizen gadflies who show up at government meetings or tipsters who think they've been wronged in some way. It's not like having a reporter there but we pay attention to them."

We had interviewed Cutter in the weeks after the June 2016 shooting that left forty-nine people dead and fifty-three hospitalized. In August, the Orlando Sheriff's Office finally released the first of the 911 calls that it received on the evening of the tragedy. Orlando police had still not released recordings of any of the calls they had received and were in a court battle with two dozen news agencies that have filed suit to get the recordings that could give a clearer picture of how police and first-responders reacted in those early minutes of the tragedy.

When the shooting broke out in Orlando, Cutter found himself in the middle of an editor's nightmare. The story broke at 2 a.m., long after the paper's deadline and after all the reporters had gone home.

A young reporter who had left for the evening was up late watching a TV movie and got the first indication something was wrong on social media. Shots had been heard in the downtown area, and streets were blocked off. Instinctively, she headed for the scene. As the story unfolded, editors were called in and more reporters headed to the scene. Before the first edition of the next day's "paper newspaper" had been put to bed, Cutter's team had filed thirty stories online and produced forty videos. The newspaper included an eight-page insert about the shooting.

"The old days of laboring to get the wording of the first sentence of your story just perfect for someone to read twelve or twenty-four hours later are gone forever," Cutter said. "You still do that but first you have to tell people what's happening in the moment. They want more than a word picture, they expect videos too. So we teach our people how to do that, how to take pictures with their phones, and social media becomes a chat room with our readers and viewers. As we began to try to identify the victims later on, social media was a great help in getting the kind of information we used to have to knock on doors to get."

Cutter covered the story with about a hundred editors and reporters, less than a third of the staff once employed by the *Sentinel*.

"Maybe because we're smaller we move quicker and we got the job done," he said. "But I do wish some of these young reporters had the opportunity I had to work more closely with editors who could help them shape a story and make it better.

"They still get edited, but not the way I worked with editors every step of the way on a story—it was the way we all learned the craft in those days. Today we just don't have that many people."

Of the many problems facing the news industry, what to do about local news is the problem that most concerns reporters and news executives throughout the profession.

At this point no one seems quite sure what will happen. No economic model has yet emerged that will ensure the financial underpinnings for the sizable staff that good, independent journalism requires. Digital advertising has provided a new revenue source, but no newspaper large or small yet makes as much off its digital service as it does off the ads in its paper newspaper.

While no solutions seem obvious, there is general agreement throughout the industry that if local newspapers go away and some entity does not rise to do what we have come to expect of them—that is, keep an eye on local government—we will experience corruption at levels we have never seen.

For all of the industry's bad news, newspapers keep finding innovative ways to keep publishing—on paper and online. Some are partnering with nonprofits and journalism schools, nearly all have devised ways to do more with less, and some, like the *Washington Post*, have been fortunate to find new owners with deep pockets, but with its new owner and new editor, the *Post* has created a whole new culture in its sparkling new headquarters. We will devote a later chapter to how the new culture has brought with it a new and different way to cover the nation's capital. With its fact checkers and veteran political reporters, the *Post* has been at the forefront of campaign coverage. The venerable *New York Times*—in addition to its new venture into video production—has shown the industry and its readers what a traditional newspaper does best: its investigative coverage into Trump campaign chief Paul Manafort's links to pro-Russian enterprises led to Manafort's resignation. Perhaps no story told more about Donald Trump's limited knowledge of foreign affairs than two interviews he gave to *Times* reporters David Sanger and Maggie Haberman. The *Times* and the *Post* led the coverage of the Russian hacking of the email systems at the Democratic National Committee. Both the *Post* and the *Times* have devoted much time and space to a critical examination of the Clinton email debacle. The *Post*'s Ellen Nakashima reported in June that the Russians had penetrated the DNC network, which was confirmed by U.S. Intelligence officials in October.

The *Times* quickly followed Nakashima's report with valuable detail and new information in the months to follow. In a seven-thousand-word December report, Sanger and *Times* reporters Eric Lipton and Scott Shane reconstructed how the hacking had taken place and the bureaucratic bumbling that occurred when the FBI tried to alert DNC officials about what was happening. (The FBI's first calls were somehow directed to the DNC "IT Help desk," where a technician did not report it to party officials fearing the calls might be a prank. Equally unbelievable, for months the FBI made no effort to alert DNC officials in person even though the DNC was a mile and a half from FBI headquarters.)

For all the problems print underwent in 2016, newspapers—where they could be found—still provided information available nowhere else to those who still chose to read them.

Chapter 5

———————O———————

And Here's the Way
We Are

New Neighbors in the News Neighborhood

AMERICANS TURNED TO MANY FAMILIAR PLACES to get their election news in 2016. Print's big two—the *New York Times* and the *Washington Post*—broke significant stories. Television network news programs no longer drew audiences as large as they did during the 1970s and 1980s, but on most weeknights, fifteen to twenty million viewers still turned to evening news broadcasts. Morning show ratings were up across the board as CBS News, after years in the morning ratings cellar, was again competitive, and guests on Sunday talk shows often set the agenda for coverage through the week. Cable news outlets tallied record audiences, and more than eighty-four million people watched the first televised debate—an all-time record. Even so, younger people were turning away from their parents' traditional news sources. For them, their phone was the place for news, just as it became the place where they organized their lives, did their shopping, found their transportation, and yes, sometimes their companions. The phone became the place to find whatever they needed, and digital news sources proliferated, as did other sites designed to fill other needs.

I began this project knowing little about this growing side of the communications landscape, and my colleague, Andrew Schwartz, has been my guide on every step of this journey. Here is his report on what he calls journalism's new digital wave.

By H. Andrew Schwartz

Our September conversation with *New York Times* columnist Maureen Dowd was one of our most-listened-to podcasts in 2016, and no wonder. No one is better at cutting to the chase than Dowd, and she offered a valuable reminder to all of us in journalism.

"With all this fragmentation and platform anxiety, we have to keep our eye on the narrative arc," she told us, "because the story is still the story whether it's by carrier pigeon or Snapchat."

Dowd is a fan of the HBO hit series *Game of Thrones*, which may explain her reference to homing birds, but in one sentence she put her finger on one of successful journalism's eternal truths: whether its delivered in *Thrones'* fictional kingdom of Westeros, during the golden years of Walter Cronkite's CBS Evening News, or in the current age of journalism's new digital wave—great story-telling and compelling content are its essential ingredients.

Dowd alluded to another factor necessary to understand the digital age: the technology that allows news to travel at warp speed also gives innovators the freedom and the ability to move quickly and make change to embrace new models in order to find an audience. That means we are only at the beginning. We should expect even more change, not less.

While surveys showed the majority of Americans still got news from television in 2016, four in ten American adults get news from digital sites, and when big stories like the election happen, in a typical week about two-thirds of U.S. adults said that they learned about the election from digital sources—news or social networking sites.

Moreover, native websites—that is, websites born on the web rather than those who evolved from print—are becoming the new normal for new generations. Here's why: digital natives—those who have spent their entire secondary education years in a country where at least half the population had access to the Internet—consume differently than older generations. According to the economist James Pomeroy, they are more likely to adopt new technology but less likely to own cars or watch television. Two-thirds of them have no landline phone.

Pomeroy estimates that there are currently 430 million digital natives worldwide, a figure that will rise to 2.3 billion by 2030.

Digitally native websites, legacy media's digital sites, and social media are the primary delivery systems of news and information for this generation. Millennials, who demographers William Strauss and Neil Howe define as born between the years 1982 to 2004, clearly consume news differently than older generations. According to a survey conducted by the American Press Institute in 2015, 82 percent of millennials get most of their news from online sources via a mixture of hard news, lifestyle news, and practical news. Pew's State of the News Media survey director Amy Mitchell told us that the number of eighteen to twenty-nine-year-olds who got their news in 2016 from social media and digitally native sites is even higher—84 percent.

To better understand journalism's new digital wave, we took a close look at three successful digitally native news and entertainment companies: Vox Media, BuzzFeed, and Mic. All three are illustrative of the modern digital news landscape.

Just a month after our discussion with Maureen Dowd, we spoke with Vox Media CEO Jim Bankoff, who told us the staff of his family of websites, or "verticals" as they are known, "understand how to grow audience and how to appeal to audience," and it shows.

The *New York Times* has called Vox Media "a publishing house for the digital age," and Digiday, a leading digital media and marketing company, calls Vox "media for millennials with jobs."

By any measure, Vox Media's audience-engagement data supports such lofty statements. Taken together, the eight media brands that make up Vox Media—Vox.com, SBNation, Eater, Racked, The Verge, Recode, Polygon, and Curbed—generate an audience of over 170 million unique monthly visitors with 880 million total monthly content views. Perhaps most tellingly, two in three Vox Media users experience Vox content on mobile devices. Content is accessed through visits to the branded websites and is also shared and consumed widely via social media platforms like Facebook and Twitter.

Bankoff's media brands, he told us, "have a voice that is unique and differentiated, that can gain an audience, so they're not just doing the same stuff that you can get elsewhere. They know how to do it in a unique way."

"That's really been the biggest key to our success. Now, we pile on top of that a healthy dose of technology and a healthy dose of understanding how to use data, so that when our talented people create something that is relevant, they can find the appropriate audiences and make sure that the content that they create garners as big an audience as possible. That's where the technology and the data comes in. Design is also a big part of it. We want it to look good. We want it to feel good. We want it to load quickly on your phones. We want it to be a great experience. So the workflow behind the technology, the design, and the data all contribute. But it starts with talent. And it starts with producing something that is relevant."

More specifically, Bankoff talks about producing content that is relevant to young adults—a key demographic when it comes to generating revenue through advertising, a critical part of Vox's business model.

"A new wave of brands have emerged like ours," Bankoff told us. "Those brands tend to have a younger audience demographic because younger audiences are growing up natively with these technologies and these platforms. And so they tend to skew more in this way. And we build brands that really speak to these audiences on these platforms the way that they were meant to be used."

Bankoff said that the age of his audience distinguishes Vox Media from cable news where the demographic is significantly older. According to Nielsen, the American company that measures media audiences, the median age of a Fox News Channel prime-time viewer is sixty-eight, and the median CNN primetime viewer is fifty-nine (during daytime, Fox's median age is sixty-seven compared to CNN's sixty-one).

"We're just telling the stories we think are relevant," Bankoff said. "But the platform is younger, the brand is new. And as a result, we have a younger audience."

We asked Bankoff why a digitally native brand such as Vox resonates with young people.

"We use this medium in different ways," Bankoff said. "We're able to tell stories. We do things in video. We do things in text. We do things in audio. And we can really take advantage of this medium in a new way. So it's a new kind of creative product too."

BuzzFeed, widely regarded as one of the most vibrant digitally native news and entertainment companies, practically invented producing and delivering the news in these "different ways" Bankoff described.

Initially cofounded in 2006 by Internet entrepreneurs Jonah Peretti, Ken Lerer, and John S. Johnson III, BuzzFeed first set out to experiment with how content goes "viral."

BuzzFeed has since grown into a global news organization and entertainment company that says it's engineered to "serve a next generation, highly engaged audience that consumes video and content across platforms, on mobile, and has an expectation that media will be relevant and connected to their lives, easily shareable, and globally accessible."

BuzzFeed may still be best known in popular culture for its viral content, which includes exploding watermelons, adorable feline photos, quizzes, and lists. But it has also evolved into an award-winning news organization headed by Ben Smith, previously a star Politico reporter and columnist who joined BuzzFeed as editor-in-chief in early 2012.

An accomplished, dogged political sleuth, Smith was one of Politico's best-known journalists due to his early mastery of communicating via Twitter. For Smith, the risk of exiting a successful news organization like Politico to work for a website peddling cat videos was not insignificant.

But Smith saw something that others didn't. He recognized that BuzzFeed could position itself as a news organization to tap into the excitement and warp speed in which social media had pushed the news cycle into overdrive.

"It was in a world where Twitter was really the center [of the news]," Smith told us on our podcast in the spring of 2016. "And so the idea of going to a place that was treating the social conversation as the front page, rather than treating the website as the front page or the print as the front page, was really appealing to me.

"It's just much more satisfying to write directly for your audience and see their response immediately and be able to engage than it is to write for a newspaper and kind of send it off and try to guess if anybody read it or hope somebody calls or writes you a letter. And particularly for political reporting, that immediacy is, I think, amazing—just really totally transforms the work."

The current scale of BuzzFeed is an incredible story. It's grown into a global media company featuring eleven international editions with seven billion global content views combined and that publishes on thirty social media platforms around the world. More than two hundred million unique visitors come to BuzzFeed.com per month.

Smith has deployed correspondents to more than half a dozen countries, has large bureaus in Washington and New York, and of course, a San Francisco bureau vigorously covering Silicon Valley. The company also has offices in cities around the world, including London, Paris, Berlin, Madrid, Sydney, Mumbai, Tokyo, Sao Paulo, Mexico City, and Toronto.

In 2016, BuzzFeed's news department and content production staff numbered over five hundred employees. By comparison, the *Washington Post's* newsroom employed more than 750 people, the *Times* stood at about 1,300, *USA Today* had 450, and *Wall Street Journal* at about 1,500.

And just like BuzzFeed, the *Post*, the *Times*, and the *Journal* hire staff with the multimedia production skills necessary to produce more engaging and sharable digital content.

Unlike BuzzFeed, the legacy newspapers aren't attempting to produce exploding watermelon videos, wacky lists, and other so-called clickbait, but they have learned a thing or two from BuzzFeed about how to make their content more accessible and compelling online.

On our podcast in the spring of 2016, the *Washington Post's* editor Marty Baron acknowledged as much, and today more than three dozen software engineers sit in the *Post* headquarters in a continuous search to find and design better and faster ways to display news content. (More on that later in this report.)

Where Smith parts ways with Baron is over the value of print. While Baron no longer believes the future of news is print, he envisions continuing the print edition of the *Post* for the foreseeable future. Smith believes print is already antiquated.

"I think that the digital tools are just unambiguously better for distributing information, for correcting errors you make," Smith said.

"Great [legacy and local] news organizations, I hope, will be able to transform themselves into digital."

For the new wave of digital news organizations like Vox Media, BuzzFeed, and Mic, print is an anathema.

Mic, with an audience that reaches more than sixty-five million millennials each month, has become the go-to media company for a generation that doesn't believe in cutting down trees to produce newspapers.

Cofounded in 2011 by millennials Chris Altchek and Jake Horowitz, Mic is a media company with a philosophical approach to gathering and reporting the news.

"Mic's approach to news is as unique as our generation (millennials)," its website declares. "Young people will define the future and we deserve a news outlet that offers quality coverage tailored to us. We are hungry for news that keeps us informed and helps us make sense of the world. Mic was founded . . . under the shared belief that millennials are inquisitive, have a healthy skepticism for conventional wisdom, and crave substantive news to spark interesting conversations. This sensibility informs everything we do."

Based in New York, Mic has about 160 people employed in offices in Stockholm, Berlin, San Francisco, Los Angeles, and Chicago. Mic has about ninety editors, writers, reporters, and video producers who report on the issues that the millennial generation cares about deeply.

Mic produces ten to thirty videos per day and publishes between fifty and one hundred articles per day. Mic cofounder Chris Altcheck told us on our podcast in the fall of 2016, just before the presidential election, that a large percentage of American millennials see or read Mic on a monthly basis (there are between seventy-five to eighty million millennials).

"As an example of how we're set up versus other newsrooms," Altcheck explained on our podcast, "we have eight editors and reporters who work exclusively on Black Lives Matter, because we believe this is a space that our generation is leading, driving, and thinks about very, very differently than our parents' generation. We have reporters and editors who focus on these sort of beats that are uniquely ours—ours, meaning generational."

We were curious as to why Altcheck thinks his generation needs its own media outlet.

"Our values in many ways are different than our parents," Altchek explained. "And our parents still run all of the biggest news brands in the world, whether it's CNN or the *New York Times* or the *Washington Post* or CBS News. The biggest, most respected news brands in the world are run by people who think about the world differently than we do.

"And then we've been lucky—and Mic has really benefited from this—our audience is at the forefront of changing the way news is consumed. So the way we think about it at Mic is our phones are the only device that matters. And our phones went from being sort of social-network-connected devices for reading articles now to—the way we think about them is our phones are hyperpersonalized TVs. Whether it's Facebook, Instagram, Snapchat, or YouTube, our users are opening their phones hundreds of times a day, opening feeds and getting very personalized video content all day long. And as a media company that's oriented exclusively towards that, we end up building our teams differently, doing our reporting differently, and it actually changes how Mic is structured in a very meaningful way. The biggest difference is, what our values are and how those values are expressed in the content formats that we've created."

So, we wondered, is there a point at which Mic caps its audience?

"Maybe," Altcheck said. "The thing we have going for us is millennials are a median age of twenty-seven. There's seventy-five to eighty million of us. We are now the biggest group of employees in the workforce. There's more of us than boomers or gen X. We're also approaching peak spending years. And so as a foundational part of the economy, millennials are by far the most important group for the next forty years. And so, as a business, that's the group you want to build your audience around. When you look at Fox News, CNN, MSNBC, all of those—all of those great news companies have a median viewer above sixty years old. That's median. That means half of them are even older than that.

"We plan on growing up with our audience," Alcheck continued. "The biggest innovation is actually improving the storytelling, improving the journalism. Our audience is maturing, is approaching a new life stage where it's about getting married and having kids and thinking about the world differently than they've been thinking about it for the last decade. And so for us, a big part of what we're doing is continuing—is a relentless focus on making our journalism better. And I think that's what's going to ultimately either keep people or people will leave. If our audience thinks that the *New York Times* is consistently doing better reporting than we are on the issues that they care about, then they will read the *New York Times*, or watch the *New York Times*. And so I think that's the bar that we hold ourselves to. And that's a lot of work.

"But on the flipside of that, we need to consistently innovate if we want to reach the next college graduates, who are twenty-one, twenty-two today, who are now on the border between millennials and gen Z. And that's where we're doing a lot of interesting things. We have built out a team that focuses exclusively on messaging and emerging apps. And so, for example, on Kik, which is a widely used chat application among high school and early college-age students in America, we have about seven hundred thousand people who interact with Mic content on a weekly basis. And that's a different form of content and it's really targeted towards younger audiences, but we're trying to bring them into the fold.

"We have launched a new app called Hyper, which is a really innovative video-only app that's performing really, really well with younger audiences. And so what we're trying to do is actually really make sure that on one side our journalism's getting better and we hold onto our current audience, and on the other side we're on these new platforms because Facebook is not that important to teenagers today. And they are consuming content on different platforms."

Which brings us to this: technology is now moving so fast it is possible to imagine a landscape where Facebook is for old people.

Mic, BuzzFeed, Vox, and others who make up the new wave of digital journalism think about that nonstop.

Journalism's New Digital Wave:
A Guide to Digitally Native News Websites

The following list is composed of the top digital-native publishers according to these guidelines:

- It must have at least ten million average monthly unique digital visitors (as of the last quarter of 2015).
- It must be born on the web—not the website of a legacy news brand.
- The outlet is a publisher of original content about news and current events.
- It is not user generated (like Facebook, Twitter, Wikipedia, Medium, or Reddit).

As we detail elsewhere in this book, all of the legacy media companies from networks and cable as well as the big newspapers have launched news-dispensing websites that are easily accessed on mobile devices. In that sense they are part of journalism's new digital wave, too.

Axios—"We have one agenda: help people get smarter, faster."[1] Launched in January 2017, Axios is a media startup that aims to redefine digital news and counter the journalism-elite stereotype. Cofounded by Jim VandeHei, former CEO and cofounder of Politico, Axios' content is concise, informative, and made to be shared on social media.

The Blaze—Based in Irving, Texas, The Blaze is a conservative news and entertainment source available on television, radio, and the Internet. Founded by talk radio personality and entrepreneur Glenn Beck, this opinion network launched in 2011.

Breitbart—Breitbart News Network is a far-right news, opinion, and commentary website founded in 2007 by conservative commentator and entrepreneur Andrew Breitbart. This controversial site gained renown by breaking news about a series of scandals involving liberal politicians, bureaucrats, and organizations. Stephen K. Bannon ran the site until he became a senior advisor to Donald Trump.

Business Insider—This German-owned American news site focuses on business with financial, tech, political, and other industry verticals. Launched in 2007, Business Insider also operates international editions in Australia, India, Malaysia, Indonesia, Singapore, China, Italy, and the UK, with local language sites in Polish and German.

Bustle—The largest digital media property aimed at millennial women, Bustle provides breaking news, entertainment, lifestyle, and fashion content. The site, self-proclaimed to be "for and by women,"[2] was founded in 2013.

BuzzFeed—This global, cross-platform social news and entertainment company is accessed through Buzzfeed.com, mobile apps, Facebook, Snapchat, YouTube, and other digital platforms. BuzzFeed is known for producing viral content, quizzes, and lists, in addition to award-winning news investigations.

The Daily Beast—Reporters and big personalities cover politics, pop culture, and world news on this original reporting and opinion site. Since it launched in 2008, the site has aimed to "avoid information overload" with smart, speedy takes.

FiveThirtyEight—Named after the number of electors in the U.S. electoral college, FiveThirtyEight uses statistical analysis, data visualization, and data-literate reporting to tell stories about politics, sports, science, economics, and culture. Statistician Nate Silver founded the site during the 2008 presidential primaries. On Election Day in 2016, more than 16.5 million unique users visited the site, spending more than 209 million minutes with the content.[3]

Huffington Post—Launched in 2005 as a group blog, Huffington Post is now a destination for content on U.S. politics, entertainment, style, world news, technology, and comedy. Political activist Arianna Huffington founded this left-leaning source.

Independent Journal Review—Founded in 2012 by entrepreneurs and former Republican Party staffers Alex Skatell and Phil Musser, IJR is a news platform and publisher designed for an "independent-minded" audience.

International Business Times—This site, with seven global editions and four different languages, provides coverage and analysis of business, economics, politics, and tech around the world. Since its founding in 2005, International Business Times has emphasized the forces that reshape the global and national economy.

Mashable—Powered by its own proprietary technology, Mashable is a source for tech, digital culture, and entertainment content. Pete Cashmore launched the site in 2005, when he was nineteen-years-old, to provide a space with up-to-date information on new social networks and software.

Mic—Mic is a news source for millennials that provides perspectives as diverse as the generation. The site covers world news, policy, technology, and science, with unique beats like Black Lives Matter.

Politico—Launched in 2007, Politico is a global news and information company at the intersection of politics and policy. It has publications based in Washington, D.C., New York, and Brussels—and is continuing to expand into various state capitals in the United States. Note: Politico was born digitally and with a print edition that it continues to produce. We included Politico on this list as an exception to our criteria because it is a news organization with a culture that was born and exists on the web.

Quartz—Born in 2012, Quartz is for business people in the new global economy. This mobile-first site is structured around a collection of what Quartz calls "Obsessions." Rather than using a fixed beats structure, Quartz's "Obsessions" cover popular phenomena and trends in real time.

Raw Story—Since its founding in 2004, Raw Story has grown from a political news site to a collaborative, investigative news nexus. Raw Story emphasizes transparency, with focal points that include Wikileaks, wiretapping, and judicial abuse.

The Root—This daily news site provides commentary on current events and culture from a variety of African American perspectives. Cofounded in 2008 by Henry Louis Gates Jr., a writer and professor of African and African American studies at Harvard, and Donald H. Graham, then owner of the *Washington Post*, the online magazine is a highbrow, political source for a primarily black audience.

Salon—When Salon began in 1995, the liberal online magazine quickly came to be seen as an embodiment of the media's future. Self-described as a "left-coast, interactive version of *The New Yorker*,"[4] the digital trailblazer covered U.S. politics, current affairs, art, and culture. In recent years, Salon has been criticized for replacing quality reporting with clickbait commentary.

Slate—Slate uses witty and entertaining writing to help readers interpret the world. Launched in 1996, this online magazine covers news, politics, technology, and culture with a focus on analyzing, rather than breaking, news.

Uproxx, "The Culture of Now"—Uproxx appeals to the digital generation. Launched in 2008, the site provides long-form and short-form news, sports, music, and entertainment content.

The Verge—Operated by Vox Media, The Verge is a multimedia effort founded in 2011 to examine how technology will change life in the future for a massive mainstream audience. The site analyzes how revolutions in media, transportation, and science have participated in modern culture.

Vox.com—Simply put, Vox.com is designed to "explain the news." Using text, original videos and podcasts, Vox.com is a destination for news, culture, and entertainment.

Vox Media—Launched in 2002, Vox Media is a portfolio of eight influential branded websites (also known as verticals): SBNation, The Verge, Polygon, Curbed, Eater, Racked, Vox, and Recode.

NOTES

1. https://www.axios.com/sp/about/#our-mission
2. https://www.bustle.com/about
3. http://espnmediazone.com/us/press-releases/2016/11/fivethirty eight-sets-traffic-records-election-day-night/
4. www.politico.com/media/story/2016/05/the-fall-of-saloncom -004551

Chapter 6

———O———

Fake News

A Clear and Present Danger

FOR THOSE OF US IN JOURNALISM, 9/11 was more than just a tragedy of monumental proportions, it was an event that helped us to understand how our role and responsibility to inform the public was changing.

Until 9/11, there was a tradition in journalism. If you made a mistake it was your responsibility to change it. If your competitor made a mistake, you ignored it and left it to your competitor to correct it.

In the new world of the web when information true, false, and in between is ricocheting around the world in real time, we learned on 9/11 the old ways would no longer do. To leave false information uncorrected even for a few minutes ran the risk of setting off pandemonium. On 9/11, once we determined information was false, we reported that, no matter where the information had come from.

Over and over that day, there were reports on the Internet that another hijacked aircraft was heading toward the Sears Tower in Chicago. In the old days we would have kept silent about the information until we had confirmed it with our own sources. If the report proved false we would have simply ignored it. But to remain silent on 9/11 could have produced mass hysteria. So it was on that awful day that a big part of the Washington Bureau's workload was to check and keep checking that report of a plane heading toward the Sears Tower.

We would knock it down, report that, and a half hour later it would pop up again, and once more we would check it out and knock it down. Our correspondent Bob Orr told me at one point, "I can't remember knocking down the same story so many times. It was like it was becoming my life's work."

Since 9/11, we have come to realize that reporting accurate information is only part of our job; equally important is our responsibility to knock down false and misleading information and to do it as quickly as possible.

Some of the false information that popped up on the web was not malicious; some items were posted just for fun.

During the administration of George W. Bush, Secretary of State Condoleezza Rice was scheduled to appear on *Face the Nation*. But after the broadcast, I found a story on the web reporting that I had been taken aback when Jerry Rice, the wide receiver for the Oakland Raiders, had shown up instead of Condoleezza Rice and that he had surprised me with his vast knowledge of foreign policy. The story of course was a joke, made up out of whole cloth, but I got emails from more than one viewer who took the spoof to be true. As is usually the case with email, some viewers liked what Jerry Rice had to say and some did not.

Spreading false and misleading information is nothing new in American politics. A quick Google check of the scurrilous accusations the Founders hurled at each other during the writing of the constitution helps us to understand that "whisper campaigns," lies, half-truths, and spin are as much a part of our campaigns as rallies, parades, bumper stickers, and yard signs.

The difference is that in the new world of instant communication, information good and bad is transmitted to millions instantly, and that can be as dangerous as it is worthwhile.

Winston Churchill said, "A lie gets halfway around the world before the truth has a chance to put its pants on." Some historians say it was actually Mark Twain who first coined that phrase, but whoever said it, it has never been truer than it is in the digital age when we are bombarded with more information true and false than any other humans who ever lived.

We asked our colleague Lucy Boyd to survey some of the far corners of the new communications landscape to determine where some of this information was coming from. Here is her report.

By Lucy Boyd

"Pope Francis Shocks World, Endorses Donald Trump for President, Releases Statement"—www.endingthefed.com

"FBI Agent Suspected in Hillary Email Leaks Found Dead in Apparent Murder-Suicide"—www.denverguardian.com

"President Obama Confirms He Will Refuse to Leave Office If Trump Is Elected"—www.burrardstreetjournal.com

"Ireland is now Officially Accepting Trump Refugees from America"—www.oppositionreport.com

Those headlines are just a handful of the fake news stories that reached voters during the 2016 presidential election. Equipped with a salacious headline, a few persuasive photographs, and a newslike format, stories like these flooded the Internet.

Toward the end of the campaign, Brian Stelter of CNN reported on just how sophisticated fake news had become. The example he used was a headline that said an anti-Trump protestor came forward claiming he was paid $3,500 to protest a Trump rally. It was a tempting story for any Trump supporter or surrogate, if only it were true. The web address for this story was ABCNews.com.co. While this may look like ABCNews.com, it is not. The .co at the end is the domain name for the country of Colombia in South America.

The story included an interview with the anti-Trump protestor who said he was recruited through an advertisement on Craigslist. He went on to describe how African Americans and Latinos were paid less than him, a Caucasian. If one keeps reading beyond the first half of the story, the authors admit they presented no real facts and created the story to prove a point. Everything about this story was completely fabricated.

This phony website was the first link that popped up in a Google search on this topic. Kellyanne Conway and Eric Trump tweeted the story out before deleting it when they realized, we assume, it was completely illegitimate, as did thousands of pro-Trump Twitter handles.

The readership that such stories can amass was underlined by a BuzzFeed analysis, which found that the top twenty false news stories of the election cycle received more "likes," "shares," and "clicks" on social media than the most popular real news stories from the top nineteen news organizations combined. When one considers that the Pew Research Center found that 62 percent of Americans get news from social media, this is a disheartening fact.

The impact that such stories had on voters is difficult to gauge, but at the least they sowed confusion.

Fake news authors are not easy to find, nor are they eager to discuss their activities. The *New York Times*, the *Washington Post*, and National Public Radio (NPR) have all run stories about people who admit to writing fake news, and from that reporting, one thing is evident: fake news can be very profitable. One former fake news writer told NPR he made between $10,000 and $30,000 per month.[1]

Fake news is a robust industry, and it works like this. First, fake news writers come up with an idea for a story based on what is happening on social media. As one fake news writer told BuzzFeed, he was so shocked by the ridiculous stories circulating on Facebook about Obama running a pedophile ring out of the White House, he wanted to test how gullible people could be. So, he made up stories meant to provoke people's emotions about topics already being discussed online.[2]

Generally, the false stories follow this pattern—eye-catching headline, interesting first paragraph, relevant photos (usually taken off the Internet), a few quotes (often not real people), and a format that looks like a typical news site (such as local weather, horoscopes, advertisements, contact pages). In some cases, the authors of the story even reveal their hoax by the end of it. For example, a story titled "Obama Signs Executive Order Banning the Pledge of Allegiance in Schools Nationwide,"[3] published October 11, 2016, on ABCnews.com.co, the same hoax website that published the story about the paid protester, discusses in its final paragraphs what happens when a "story like this goes viral" in the context of advertisements and social media.

For fake news publishers, the more viral, the better. Advertising revenue depends on how many eyeballs see the advertisements on the fake news webpage. With advertising systems like Google's AdSense, it takes a few simple clicks to start selling advertising space on a website. Once the webpage registers with AdSense, Google selects advertisements based on the demographics of the audience. As a young female professional, I may see clothing or weekend getaway ads while a middle-aged father of two may see SUV or home loan ads. What we found surprising is that consumers do not have to click on the advertisement for it to make money—as long as they see it, Google and the fake news publisher can cash in.

This is where social media becomes essential for the fake news industry. An inflammatory story with advertisements remains on the dark fringes of the Internet unless it disseminates to a wider audience. On Facebook, fake news publishers buy cheap advertising space to promote their headline. Another technique is to drop the article into a hyperpartisan Facebook group that they think would be receptive to the story.

Dissemination is also made possible through Twitterbots. Twitterbots are computer software programmed to automatically tweet, retweet, like, and follow other users on Twitter. Twitterbots are made to look like real people complete with a name, a picture, and sometimes even a biography. One can identify Twitterbots by the rapid rate or inhuman pattern by which they tweet and retweet.

Twitterbots have been found to tweet out and retweet fake news stories that align with their political agenda. One such story pushed by Twitterbots was the pizzagate conspiracy, a story that falsely claimed there was a child sex trafficking ring in Washington, D.C., run by Democrats and Hillary Clinton. With "#pizzagate" as its rallying flag, Twitterbots were programmed to tweet and retweet any message that contained that hashtag. As Twitterbots retweeted by the thousands, the conspiracy was artificially inflated to look much more popular than it actually was, which caught the attention of real people, or in the case of #pizzagate, Edgar Welch.

Fake news is fake news until it becomes dangerous. On December 5, 2016, Edgar Welch, a North Carolinian with two children, walked into a Northwest Washington, D.C., pizza restaurant armed with an assault weapon. Welch searched the restaurant, and at one point, shot the lock off a closet where, much to his surprise, he found no children. He told police he was there to "self-investigate" a story he saw on the web describing a child pedophile ring run by Hillary Clinton and other Democrats that was operating out of the restaurant's basement. The story was completely false and thoroughly discredited by law enforcement authorities (the restaurant doesn't even have a basement). In fact, when Welch left the restaurant to surrender to police, he admitted that he did not find what he came looking for.[4] Despite this, the story continues to circulate on the Internet.

Fortunately, there were no injuries and the man was arrested. But the story didn't stop there. Within a few days, new reports began to circulate alleging that Edgar Welch was an actor hired by authorities to discredit the original child sex scandal story.

Months after the incident, the pizza restaurant owner is still getting death threats.

In another incident, a woman named Lucy Richards was arrested for threatening the parents of a six-year-old murdered in the Newtown tragedy at Sandy Hook Elementary School. Federal authorities said Ms. Richards believed the story was a hoax, and she wasn't the only one. Entire web blogs are dedicated to proving that Sandy Hook was "staged."

Conspiracy theories are not new and have been circulating long before the rise of individual blogs and social media. Richard Hofstadter's 1965 book *The Paranoid Style in American Politics* traces the many conspiracies circulated throughout American history. In the nineteenth century, anti-Catholic groups coalesced around a belief that European countries and even the Pope himself were trying to upend their Protestant way of life by sending Catholic immigrants to America in droves.

And of course, McCarthyism during the Cold War promulgated the idea that the Kremlin had infiltrated not only our society but also the government as they sought total world domination. McCarthy said of Secretary of State George Marshall, a leader in the World War II Allied victory, that "his decisions, maintained with great stubbornness and skill, always and invariably served the world policy of the Kremlin."[5] George Marshall was the Army Chief of Staff during World War II, and later, as Secretary of State, the man who designed the Marshall Plan, which was responsible for the economic recovery of Western Europe after the war. Serving the Kremlin would not only have been logistically difficult but also severely against his own interests.

No clear answer exists as to why some individuals are prone to conspiracy theories and others are not. There is a considerable amount of literature, however, on common characteristics of a conspiracy-leaning mindset. Among many others, Hofstadter points out the following characteristics about conspiracy theorists: "Since what is at stake is always a conflict between absolute good and absolute evil, the quality needed is not a willingness to compromise but the will to fight things out to a finish." Research by Viren Swami found that conspiracy theories are often used by those who feel powerless or uncertain.[6] This is why most disasters, whether it is tornados in Oklahoma (Obama did it) or the Sandy Hook school shooting tragedy (staged), are immediately followed by conspiracy stories and a social media frenzy. If people face uncontrollable situations, they attribute responsibility to a high level of coordination without considering the possibilities of randomness, coincidence, or one indescribably insane individual.

Facts and evidence have never been persuasive for those prone to believing in conspiracies, which may explain why Trump stuck to his false claim that Barack Obama was not born in the United States until September 2016, only to replace it with a new theory: the Clinton campaign started the birther rumors in 2008.

The persistence of the birther movement is congruent with research that finds a "backfire effect"—when evidence is provided to prove political misinformation wrong, it only serves to strengthen the ideological person's belief in the falsehood.[7] Despite the fact that President Obama presented his birth certificate in the beginning of his presidency, social media and fake news sites still report he is not an American. It begs the question, then, what can the media do in terms of fact checking if birth certificates no longer prove citizenship?

The devolution of the truth took an unexpected turn in the fall of 2016. As Trump dipped in the polls, he began planting the seeds for a "rigged election." He threatened the smooth transition of power in American elections that are the envy of the world. He claimed with no discernable evidence that voter fraud was rampant and charged that vast conspiracies—the international banks, politicians, the media—everyone but Putin—were plotting against him. Reporters are used to be being blamed for a variety of sins, but accusations of being in cahoots with international banks is a new one.

Whether his objective was to lay the groundwork for a loss or he truly believed the election was rigged, when Trump refused during the final debate to say whether he would accept the results of the election, it shocked viewers across America. No candidate in recent memory has ever said such a thing, and in a commentary after the debate Bob Schieffer said, "This is simply not how we do things in the United States."

There is a bit of nuance here that should be acknowledged. In many past elections, the losing party has often accused the other party of a rigged election. According to a Fairleigh Dickinson Poll, 37 percent of Democrats believed Republicans committed election fraud in 2004 to keep the White House. The same poll finds that in 2012, 36 percent of Republicans thought Democrats did the same.[8] The difference in 2016 was the fact that the party nominee willingly promoted such a belief.

When asked about the conspiracy theories advanced by Donald Trump and why they appeal to many of his supporters, conservative radio host and author Hugh Hewitt offered this explanation: "I believe Mr. Trump has tapped into an enormously potent force in American history—American populism. Richard Hofstadter called it the paranoid impulse in American politics, but I think it's just actually basic populism. 'Nobody hears me. Nobody cares about me.' Donald Trump arrives, and though he's a billionaire and builds these enormously successful hotels and buildings, he understands the little guy because he's around working men—working men and women. That's what I think the basic mindset is."

Fake news comes from both the left and the right. In October 2015, an email began circulating with an image of Donald Trump on what appeared to be a page from *People* magazine. The headline quoted Trump as saying that if he ever ran for president, it would be as a Republican because they are the "dumbest group of voters in the country."

The image was shared extensively on Twitter and Facebook, but there was only one problem. The interview with *People* never happened, and Trump never said such a thing. Even after it was debunked by various fact checkers and *People* itself, the image and quote pervaded the Twitter-verse well into 2016.[9]

Since inauguration, left-leaning fake news stories have gained prominence on social media. A story about Neil Gorsuch, Trump's Supreme Court nominee, claimed he founded a club in college called the "Fascism Forever Club" (not true). Another story, dressed up with video borrowed from a 2007 HBO documentary titled "Police Raid Standing Rock Camp, Dismantle Tipis and Are Burning What Remains" received three hundred thousand shares on Facebook. The psychological explanation offered is that when desperate, people will believe anything, and since Trump became president, some liberals are desperate.

At first, Facebook, Google, and Twitter were reluctant to respond to criticism that they themselves play a role in the fake news industry, much less had any effect on the election results. To be clear, it is impossible to say whether fake news changed the outcome of the election, and a Stanford study published in January 2017 serves as further proof that it did not.[10] Nonetheless, after heated criticism, all three have made changes in an attempt to stifle the proliferation of fake news on their platforms and search engines.

Facebook's proposals include efforts to work with reputable fact checkers to flag stories as false, allow users to identify misinformation, and prohibit hoax websites from buying advertising space on Facebook to showcase their provocative headline. In March 2017, Facebook started alerting users to articles that were "in dispute" by the Associated Press and Snopes.com. It is an imperfect system—users can still choose to spread the fake news, and not every questionable article is yet labeled, but the environment is shifting.

Google says it is prohibiting spoof websites from using their AdSense advertising tools that allow for targeted advertising at a low cost. As of spring 2017, Google has stopped two hundred fake news websites from using their AdSense tools. Stifling the economic incentives is not enough to some critics, who point out that the Google search bar leads people to conspiracies and fake news through its autocomplete feature. For example, when I type in "Sandy Hook," Google automatically fills in "Sandy Hook Fake" in the drop-down menu of four options. For others, "Sandy Hook Hoax" and "Sandy Hook Conspiracy" auto-complete because everyone's search is personalized.[11] In behavioral science, it has been found that choice architecture, or the way options are presented to people, can influence the decisions people end up making. Google often says they are always working to improve their algorithms because it is based on dynamic user data. This begs the question though: Will we always play catchup, or will we ever get it right?

Facebook CEO and founder Mark Zuckerberg has said repeatedly he does not believe Facebook should be the "arbiter of truth" and that this is a complicated issue of technology and standards. It is one thing to block blatantly fake news, but what about hyperpartisan bias? Parody? Satire? Individual rants? What is free speech and what is not? As Facebook becomes a news source for more and more American adults (remember, that number is at 62 percent currently), the company will continue to face these difficult decisions. What cannot be disputed is that the consequences of these fake reports are real. James Alefantis, owner of the Comet Ping Pong Pizzeria, which was attacked by the conspiracy theorist with the AK-15 in December 2016, hired security guards because of the persistent death threats. Months after the incident had been thoroughly discredited, fifty demonstrators showed up near the White House demanding an investigation of the fabricated sex trafficking ring. The *Washington Post* quoted one demonstrator as saying, "I don't have any doubt that Pizzagate is real."

Much of the criticism so far has been directed at the distributors of content and social media, but news consumers must also accept that some of the responsibility for knocking down fake news rests with them. A quick Google search can often resolve questions about the validity of questionable stories. Performing a reverse image search will tell us whether *People* magazine ever actually published a photo of Donald Trump saying Republicans were dumb. Even simple acts like reading to the end of a suspicious article may reveal its intention to fool us. Unfortunately, with increasing polarization and hyperpartisanship, it is easy to believe what seems to confirm our point of view. As one former fake news writer told 60 Minutes, if it is in a news-ish format and agrees with preexisting biases, people will believe just about anything.[12]

Over and over again in 2016, examples such as these have shown us that the first rule for using the Internet to gather news is "buyer beware." Conspiracies and nefarious false stories have existed on the fringes of society for centuries, but now we have it all at our fingertips—archived and organized by partisan slant, popularity, and medium. The Internet has become an ideal platform for making misinformation look official. Social media is an ideal (and free) distributor of such information. As we saw in the 2016 election, this combination can become a contagious environment for stories that validate our ideological interests but are nowhere near the truth.

Every day we discover more benefits of digital media, and its possibilities are endless, but as Schieffer has pointed out, there is also a downside.

"Now," he told a Harvard seminar, "the nuts can all find each other."

NOTES

1. http://www.npr.org/sections/alltechconsidered/2016/11/23/503146770/npr-finds-the-head-of-a-covert-fake-news-operation-in-the-suburbs

2. https://www.buzzfeed.com/craigsilverman/this-website-just-showed-its-still-super-easy-is-to-get-traf?utm_term=.jfXepA0RV#.ncVJdWO0K

3. https://web.archive.org/web/20161012021029/http://abcnews.com.co/

4. https://assets.documentcloud.org/documents/3237677/Welch-Edgar-Federal-Complaint-Dec-2016.pdf

5. Richard Hofstadter, The Paranoid Style of American Politics: An Essay (New York: Penguin Random House, 1965).

6. Viren Swami, "Social Psychological Origins of Conspiracy Theories: The Case of the Jewish Conspiracy Theory in Malaysia," Frontiers in Psychology 3 (2012): 280.

7. Jason Reifler and Brendan Nyhan, "When Corrections Fail: The Persistence of Political Misperceptions," Dartmouth College, http://www.dartmouth.edu/~nyhan/nyhan-reifler.pdf.

8. https://www.scribd.com/document/120815791/Fairleigh-Dickinson-poll-on-conspiracy-theories

9. Ishmael N. Daro, "No, Trump Never Told People Magazine That Republicans Are 'The Dumbest' Voters," Buzzfeed.com, July 2016, https://www.buzzfeed.com/ishmaeldaro/trump-fake-quote-people-magazine?utm_term=.blq5bb5BB5#.mkAZDDZzzZ.

10. https://web.stanford.edu/~gentzkow/research/fakenews.pdf

11. https://www.theguardian.com/technology/2016/dec/16/google-autocomplete-rightwing-bias-algorithm-political-propaganda

12. Segment that aired March 26, 2016, called "Fake News" with Scott Pelley.

Part Two

───────────○───────────

THE FUTURE
HAS ARRIVED

OLD DOGS HAD TO LEARN NEW TRICKS as the changes forced by digital brought a new culture to big-city newsrooms. As local newspapers nationwide continued to close, new organizations arose to fill the void. Americans got their news from many places, some familiar, some not. New strategies to deliver the news became the norm for those news companies that survived.

Chapter 7

———○———

Walt Mossberg
Bridging the Gap

WALT MOSSBERG, THE CRUSTY FORMER COLUMNIST for the *Wall Street Journal*, is the poster child for how journalists are adapting to the new digital age.

He reminds me of a bridge—a specific bridge, the one in Istanbul that connects East and West, Europe and Asia.

More than any journalist I know, Mossberg, the former *Wall Street Journal* National Security Correspondent, straddles the old journalism and the new, one foot firmly in the old world of newspapers and the other firmly anchored in the world of technological change and websites.

His professional journey is as good a guide as I've found to the new era and a roadmap for all of us—journalists and consumers of journalism—who are trying to understand this complex new world in which we all find ourselves.

First some background: after covering national and international affairs at the *Journal* for eighteen years as Pentagon correspondent, deputy Washington Bureau chief, chief international economics writer, and other key Washington Bureau jobs, he went to *Journal* managing editor Norman Pearlstine in 1990 and said, "I don't want to do this anymore."

When the somewhat startled Pearlstine said, "What do you want to do?" Mossberg said, "I want to write a column about computers."

Mossberg had no science background but had become so fascinated with computers they became his hobby, and he was convinced they were becoming the next big thing.

Pearlstine was interested, but he had bigger fish to fry on his news stove. He was convinced communism was about to collapse and told Mossberg with that world-changing event looming, he couldn't take him off the national security beat.

Mossberg agreed with Pearlstine's analysis, so they struck a deal. If he would stay on national security one more year, Pearlstine would let him begin the column on a six-month trial basis.

"After six months, if people don't like it," Pearlstine told him, "I'm going to kill it. If it's popular, you can keep doing it."

Pearlstine kept his word. Communism collapsed as if on cue, and Mossberg began the column in 1991. It became one of the *Journal's* most popular features. That led to his partnering with another *Journal* columnist, Kara Swisher, to create AllThingsD.com, a website devoted to tech coverage. The *Journal's* parent company owned the website; Mossberg and Swisher ran it.

Mossberg continued writing the column until 2013, when he and Swisher left the *Journal* to found and run Recode, a tech website that earned a reputation for breaking big stories out of Silicon Valley.

In 2015 Mossberg sold Recode to Vox Media, an all-stock transaction estimated at the time at $15 to $20 million but now may be worth twice that. Mossberg became executive editor at The Verge, Vox Media's tech website. He still writes the column, often appears on radio and television, and was given the prestigious Loeb Award for commentary, the first technology journalist to receive such an award.

Mossberg believes there is no better time than now to become a journalist, "especially for those with an entrepreneurial bent because you can start a website in about ten minutes with no background in technology."

Ask Mossberg the key question about the state of journalism, "Has all the new information made us more informed?" and you get a somewhat nuanced response. He remembers back to the day in the preweb CompuServe era when he said to his wife: "'Oh my God.

I can look up something in Poland from our basement!' And of course it's much better than that now but the point is, we have much more at our fingertips now but we have much worse curation.

"What," he asks rhetorically, "was a newspaper? What is a newspaper? What is a nightly newscast, local newscast? They've curated bunches of news stories, journalism. Encyclopedia Britannica was a curated attempt to capture most of the basic knowledge you would need about the world. Today we have way more journalists, way more information providers, and way less curation."

In other words, we have more information, but it's sometimes harder to find, a lot harder in some cases.

What advice does he have for struggling newspapers?

"All of them should basically redefine themselves as digital organizations, with a print expression of the news almost as a sideline for the dwindling number of people that want to take the print edition and the dwindling number of advertisers that want to be there," he said. "It's probably still more profitable. You'd be surprised at how hard it is to make money on the web.

"They should just be a website. I'm not saying they should stop printing the paper, but they should think of the paper as an ancillary business. They should be doing podcasts. They should be doing web videos, Facebook video, Twitter video."

Even so, the technology is changing so fast that even a website is becoming obsolete. As Mossberg pointed out to us, Facebook, Google, and Apple have all started news platforms, and content providers are redoing their stories to run instantly on them, particularly on Facebook, without linking back to the website.

This so-called off-platform publishing is lucrative for economic and wider circulation reasons, but it brings with it certain dangers. "Facebook right now and Apple and the other guys are giving the publishers very good deals in the advertising splits and all that. But that could change," he says. "So, you're at the mercy of Facebook. If that's where your traffic is coming from and they decide to change the rules, you're screwed."

He also sees a greater danger in so much power being concentrated in such a small group of people.

Mossberg says he knows the people running the big technology companies and they all understand the value of a vibrant press, but it may not always be that way. "They are all in business just like the publishers," he said. "We're all in business. Let's not forget we've had a lot of bad publishers, even in the glory days before the Internet. We had about 1,700, 1,800 papers when I started as a reporter and 1,500 of them were mostly garbage—if an idealistic reporter wanted to write a story about how a local car dealer was ripping off the public and the car dealer was the newspaper's biggest advertiser, a lot of those papers would have killed the story.

"So, it's not like those days were holy and now it's awful.

"Having said that, we've never quite seen the experience we're beginning to see now—that some of the publishing decisions and architecture underlining it may be in the hands of somebody who has nothing to do with the website and doesn't employ the reporter.

"I think it could have profound implications for democracy to put that much power into the hands of a handful of companies, organically that's just a scary thought."

Another scary thought at least to some is also on Mossberg's radar these days—artificial intelligence, teaching machines to think.

It's the biggest thing on Silicon Valley's plate these days.

"It's called machine learning," he said. "Facebook, Apple, and Google are all deeply into it. iPhone has Siri, that's a crude version of artificial intelligence.

"Amazon has a device called Echo that sits in your home waiting for you to ask a question, sports scores, you can ask for a flash briefing and get the short NPR newscast. You can ask for recipes, set a timer."

Echo's Siri is a voice that answers to the name Alexa, and her significance in the new world was underlined in December 2016 when an Arkansas prosecutor investigating a murder subpoenaed an Echo device. Basically, the prosecutor wanted to ask Alexa if she had heard anything on the night a dead man was found face down in a friend's hot tub. Amazon resisted handing over the device on privacy grounds.

"We're in the very early innings of this," Mossberg said, "but this is what everyone in Silicon Valley is working on."

Mossberg believes the coming of the Internet has changed our culture profoundly, mostly for the better but not always. He believes privacy has been redefined and that our culture has been coarsened. "It's hard to know how much it has changed while we're in the middle of it, and we're in the middle of it," he told me.

Not many would quarrel with that, but unlike so many in journalism, he can take pride in one thing: he saw it coming.

Chapter 8

───────○───────

The *Washington Post*
New Culture, New Ways

IF THERE IS ONE NEWSPAPER that is doing what every newspaper wishes it could, it is the *Washington Post*.

Post editor Martin Baron has been dealt a good hand, and he's playing it very well. As newspaper ad revenues continue to decline and other editors reduce staff, Baron has what no other newspaper has, a billionaire owner, Jeff Bezos. With Bezos's financial backing and a commitment to make the *Post* America's best newspaper, the venerable *Post* has moved into a new and impressive state-of-the art headquarters, hired sixty new reporters and newsroom support staff, and created a new rapid-response investigative unit. The team covering the White House will now number seven (count 'em) reporters, a duty handled by a single reporter, Carroll Kilpatrick, in the Watergate Days. (Carl Bernstein and Bob Woodward never set foot in a White House press briefing.)

Bezos has allowed Baron to change not just the way the *Post* does things but to create an entirely new newsroom culture.

When *Post* employees and other Washington luminaries celebrated the opening of the *Post*'s new headquarters on January 28, 2016, Bezos told the crowd, "We're not just trying to make money. We think this is important." But he also said, "This needs to be a sustainable business because that's healthy for the mission."

By December 2016, it was becoming clear that Bezos was getting what he needed; word spread through the newsroom that the

Post had finished the year in the black. Publisher Fred Ryan made it official in an internal memo just before Christmas: the *Post* was "profitable and growing," he reported. New subscribers had increased 75 percent as digital subscription revenue doubled. Under the leadership of Ryan, whom Bezos hired two years ago, and Baron, the last editor hired by the Graham family, what was once just a newspaper has evolved into a media company. Or as Baron would put it, "a journalism company." (He hates words like *media* and *content* and says "journalism is what we do.") Today, the *Post* not only publishes a newspaper printed on paper but also a 24/7 digital product on its website that includes bulletin alerts, analysis, video packages that reach readers and viewers on their phones, newsletters, summaries, and charts, all tailored for phone and tablet as well as running commentary during major events such as the presidential debates.

Baron loves newspapers, but he has brought a new attitude about them to the *Post*. He is not even sure how long they will be around in their current form. When Andrew Schwartz and I talked to him in June 2016, he made a statement that few newspaper people would have made ten years ago.

"We have to recognize that print does not represent the future of the news business," he said. "We live in a digital society. We really live in a mobile society. Everybody expects that they should be able to get any news at any time, wherever they are on a device that fits into a pocket. And they can get that kind of information.

"It's projected that within four years something like 80 percent of the world's population will have access to a smartphone. That's amazing. The world has changed, and we have to change with it."

Baron admits that he and his team put more emphasis now on the digital product than the paper version of the *Post*, and in October 2015, the *Post* moved ahead of the *New York Times* in web traffic for the first time. Since then, the two companies have jockeyed back and forth for the lead. In October 2016, the *Post* reached an astonishing 106 million viewers online and topped that with 107 million in November. Not all are subscribers, of course, but subscriptions are up sharply. In a study conducted earlier last year,

Northeastern University professor Dan Kennedy cited statistics showing that CNN.com was the only American news site getting more page views than the *Post*.

The bad news is that while online readership is growing, as it is with nearly all other newspapers, print circulation is nowhere near what it once was. *Post* daily circulation has gone from a peak of 832,000 to 432,000. Since 2008, the Sunday paper has dropped from 881,000 to 572,000.

The difficulty of finding a business model to support newspapers is underlined by the fact that even with declining revenues from print, newspapers still make more off print advertising than digital.

When Baron arrived at the *Post* January 1, 2013, six months before the Graham family announced they were selling the paper to Bezos, he was already one of the country's premier editors. He had come from the *Boston Globe*, where he led the paper's stunning expose of the Catholic Church coverup of pedophile cases involving priests in the Boston area—a story that won a Pulitzer and later became the Oscar-winning movie *Spotlight*.

From Baron himself to legendary Watergate reporter Bob Woodward and the newest hires, the Graham family's decision to sell the newspaper left *Post*ies shaken, but today it is hard to find anyone at the *Post*, including Woodward, who believes the sale was a mistake.

Even with the newhires who will be joining the *Post* in 2017, the staff still will not be as large as it was at its peak in the 1990s, but there will be more people in the newsroom than at the time of Watergate. As Baron points out, there is much more to do.

"We're not just publishing a newspaper once or twice a day," he told us. "We are a 24/7 news operation. We have to provide news wherever it happens and provide it almost instantaneously.

"We're also doing video and audio and social media, you name it. So there are a lot of responsibilities that exist today that did not exist at the time of Watergate."

Baron says he now has an active and thriving video department, a graphics department that focuses on interactive techniques, and new storytelling forms.

The company also has dozens of designers and computer engineers who are constantly looking for new ways and better digital platforms to present the news.

Baron knows that the *Post* is in a unique place. It has a sound financial base, and it is located in the nation's capital, which makes national news local news. But what he has learned should be of value to news organizations that have not been so fortunate. Lesson one: It is not the platform that makes it all work—it's the content that appears on those platforms.

The Internet age was just dawning when Leslie Moonves, the chairman of the CBS Corporation, told me, "Remember this: if it's no good on the big screen, it's no good on a small screen."

Baron couldn't agree more, and he has concluded each platform must be treated differently.

As he explains it: "The web is a different medium. We had newspapers. Then along came radio. Radio's different from print. You don't read a newspaper on the radio. Then along comes television. You don't read a radio story on television. You have your own distinct communication on TV.

"Then along comes the web. Our first instinct was to put a newspaper story on the web. Then, we said, that's not enough. Let's put it up faster. And we did. What we really needed to do and what we are doing is rethinking the storytelling process in an environment where the web is its own medium, and in fact, mobile may be its own medium too.

"So that is a style that conveys a greater level of authenticity where you hear the voice—I think it's more authentic when you hear the voice of the writer more—where there's more personality in the writing, where it's more casual, more conversational. It's more accessible, it makes use of the tools we have available to us now—video, and audio and social media and original documents and animations. We have a wide variety of tools, and we're trying to use them all."

Nothing better underlines Baron's philosophy than The Fix, one of the *Post* franchises started by forty-year-old Chris Cillizza as a blog in 2006. Cillizza left the *Post* for CNN in March 2017, but the *Post* will continue the feature with a team of five that turns out a variety of features, a column, an electronic newsletter "The

5-Minute Fix" run by reporters Amber Phillips and Terri Rupar that has eighty thousand subscribers, and a podcast.

During the presidential debates, Cillizza and his crew got seven and a half million unique visitors and at times generated more web traffic than the website Politico.

Cillizza set the tone for the feature with a breezy, conversational style, and during big events he offered instant analysis and running commentary.

He came into journalism when reporters wrote the "who, what, when, where and how" one day and saved the analysis for the next edition.

"Now," he says, "people want their news and analysis simultaneously. There's no break. They watch the debate, they look at Twitter. When it ends they want someone to tell them, 'I thought this was good, I thought this was bad.'"

Cillizza is aware of the danger that is posed by mixing opinion and fact, and some of his colleagues at the *Post* were "not thrilled with my concept of news," as he put it. But in the new era when people learn from multiple sources what has just happened, he believes news organizations should devote as much time and resources to the "why" of a news story as it does to the "what."

The *Post* still holds to the journalistic tradition of separating fact and opinion and labeling opinion as such except on its editorial and op-ed pages, but when Baron talks about the challenges facing metropolitan dailies, to me, much of what he says reflects Cillizza's thinking.

"Each newspaper must figure out what fortifies its bond with the community. How do they become essential to the people who live in their region? What are the subjects they absolutely must know? What do they depend on you for? Those are the kinds of questions that have to be asked and have to be answered." In other words, understanding local readers' needs and explaining the "why" of local stories.

Campaign 2016 was an unusual election season to be sure, but it gave Baron and his team a chance to put their new way of doing things into practice, and no single news organization covered the story better.

Campaign beat reporters were consistently ahead of or at least equal to their competitors, reporter David Fahrenthold broke numerous stories, especially on Donald Trump's finances. He tracked down fascinating revelations about Trump's charitable giving. Dan Balz, who has become the dean of political reporters since the passing of *Post* reporter David Broder, provided thought-provoking analysis, Cillizza's franchise produced smart insight, columnist Dana Milbank offered trenchant yet witty commentary, and *Post* factchecker Glenn Kessler was as good or better than anyone else on his beat. The *Post* editorial and op-ed pages remained the liveliest of the major newspapers. David Ignatius consistently provided insight on foreign policy available nowhere else. Across the political spectrum, E. J. Dionne and Eugene Robinson on the left, and Ruth Marcus on the center left, were balanced by George Will, Kathleen Parker, Jennifer Rubin, and Michael Gerson on the right. Gerson, a former speechwriter for George W. Bush, especially, was at the top of his game. The addition of Margaret Sullivan's media column became must reading in the industry. The *Post* editorial board, as did most newspapers, endorsed Clinton, but their editorials were as tough on her as they were on Trump.

When we interviewed Baron for this study, he talked about the *Post*'s "customer engagement funnel," which sounded like some sort of public relations term. I laughed and said, "What in the world is that?" Baron let me know he was dead serious, and it was a concept that was first, not unique to the *Post*, and second, what he believes is the key to the *Post*'s success.

Here is the way he sees *Post* customers: At the top of the funnel are casual viewers, not necessarily people who are even looking for news but people who may have seen a link to a *Post* story on social media, most likely Facebook, or even on a friend's email.

If that person clicks on the *Post* link, he or she may not only read that story but also be exposed to others that draw the reader deeper into the funnel. This, Bezos and Baron believe, will cause people to develop a habit of visiting the *Post* more often. Eventually, as they are drawn deeper into the funnel, some of them will decide to pay for a subscription to the *Post*'s "digital bundle."

As Baron told Northeastern University professor Dan Kennedy, who is writing a book on the influence of billionaires on the news business, "The goal is to widen the top of the funnel as much as possible by maximizing total digital traffic and converting some small percentage of that traffic into loyal, subscription-buying customers." Widening the top of the funnel—seeking out more and more platforms such as putting content on Facebook Instant articles— has made the *Post* more of a true national newspaper and to a lesser but growing extent a newspaper of international influence.

In the end, Baron told us, it still comes down to marrying the latest technology to content, "journalism" as he likes to call it.

The overriding question is, can the business model under which the *Post* is operating generate the same levels of revenue in a non-election year as it did in 2016? In his research paper, Professor Kennedy wrote: "If the *Post* is to succeed the success will be based on three ingredients: (a) outstanding journalism, especially on national and international issues, (b) a large and growing digital audience and (c) a strategy to convert that audience into enough revenue through digital subscriptions and advertising. The first two ingredients are already in place, the third is as much of a challenge at the *Post* as it is in the rest of the beleaguered newspaper business."

The good news for all of journalism is that so far at the *Post*, it's working.

Chapter 9

———————O———————

The *New York Times*
Doing What They Do Best (but Faster)

THE TIMES THEY ARE A-CHANGING.

Being a morning paper, people didn't start wandering into the *New York Times* Washington Bureau until midmorning or so in the old days—first there was coffee, checking messages, and other mundane matters, but things really didn't get themselves organized until around noon when editors would confer with the bosses in New York and discuss the stories to be covered.

By one o'clock, the beat reporters were off on their rounds, and the big guns like super columnist Scotty Reston were smoozing sources at restaurants like Provencal and San Souci. By late afternoon, stories began coming together, and writers facing a six or seven o'clock deadline sat down to their typewriters to turn out their stories for the next day's paper. They wrote one story a day, turned it in, and departed for drinks with colleagues, then went home to family or other pursuits. The next day they would do it all over again.

To quote Poe's famous raven: "Nevermore!"

"And no way, no how," adds Elisabeth Bumiller, the feisty *Times* Bureau chief.

When Bumiller sent out a memo announcing the *Times* was expanding the team covering the White House to six reporters, old *Time*rs reminded her they used to get by with two.

"I responded, 'Have you ever heard of something called the Internet'?" Bumiller chuckled.

The increased workload brought on by the web (reporters may file five or six stories daily) and the unpredictability of the new administration has the Washington Bureau on a whole new schedule. Bumiller's team now has one White House correspondent and an editor on Tweet patrol beginning at 6 a.m. Under the current plan, two correspondents will cover daily happenings on a morning shift and through the day; two more will come on duty at midafternoon and stay through midnight. The other two will work on longer-range stories. The correspondents will rotate from one shift to another on a regular schedule. The *Times* will also have an investigative team looking at all aspects of the administration.

Bumiller makes no bones about it: readers may question why reporters pay so much attention to Tweets, but she sees them as a new way for officials to communicate that can't be ignored.

"He's the president of the United States," she says. "We look at the Tweets the way we look at White House press releases. Some we ignore, some we realize are news."

On the morning we interviewed her, she noted that Trump had sent out five Tweets between 6 and 7 a.m., including one in which he revived his campaign allegation that "Hillary Clinton was guilty as hell."

In the old days, the *Times* would take no notice of such items until the next day's paper.

Under the new way of doing business, that item will go directly to Briefing Editor Jonathan Weisman. He takes such news along with other breaking stories and publishes them in a running feature online. Such features, which have come to be called newsletters, have proven to be popular not only with *Times*'s readers but also across the web.

Bumiller estimates that reporters may contribute to five or six such summaries during the day before they begin to shape the story that will appear in the next day's paper.

Several blocks away at the *Washington Post*, Executive Editor Martin Baron admits the web now takes priority over the paper edition of his newspaper. Bumiller is not ready to go that far, but she says there is equal emphasis on both. There is no question where the growth has come.

Despite the new president's effort to picture the *Times* as "failing," *Times* people, like those at the *Post*, report phenomenal growth.

The *Times*'s digital reach has risen to a new high of 1.5 to 1.6 million daily, Bumiller says, while the print audience is around six hundred thousand to seven hundred thousand. The good news surprised even the *Times*'s top editor Dean Baquet.

"I remember going to a celebration not that long ago when we crossed a million and that seemed like such an elusive, big thing, and if we have more years like the year we just had, I don't think that . . . ten million subscribers is unreasonable," he told *Times*'s Public Editor Liz Spayd.

For all the innovation, the *Times*'s great strength remains its huge corps of reporters—experts in a variety of fields who have the ability to penetrate the most hardened bureaucracies and the courage to publish information that is in the public interest.

There is no better example of what newspapers and especially the *Times* do best than the long interviews that *Times* correspondents Maggie Haberman and David Sanger conducted with candidate Donald Trump.

During the March 26 interview, Trump had a jarringly flip tone when asked if he would honor the NATO commitment to defend tiny Estonia if Russia moved in.

"Yeah, I would," he said. "It's a treaty. It's there. We defend everybody (he laughs) we defend everybody. We're defending the world . . . we owe 19 billion dollars, it will soon be 21 trillion. But we defend everybody. When in doubt come to the United States, we'll defend you, sometimes free of charge."

While it was sometimes difficult to follow Trump's long, often unformed sentences, the questions were elegant in their simplicity. There were no gotchas, no reporters jumping from behind a door to stick a microphone in someone's face, just intelligent, well thought out, basic, direct questions with obvious follow-ups, as when Maggie Haberman asked, during the first interview, "Would you object if they (Japan and South Korea) got their own nuclear arsenal given the threat they face from North Korea and China?"

That question drew a long, disjoined answer from Trump, but he conceded it might become necessary. In part he said, "Every time North Korea raises its head we get calls from Japan and everybody else, 'do something,' and there'll be a point at which we're just not going to be able to do it anymore. Now does that mean nuclear? It could mean nuclear."

Later he added, "When we made these deals we were a rich country. We're not a rich country anymore." He then added this: "I would rather—(with) North Korea having them—Japan having them also. You may well be better off if that's the case."

Translation: The treaty that places Japan under America's nuclear umbrella and declares that an attack on Japan is an attack on America has become too expensive—too one-sided. Japan should go nuclear.

In the second interview in July, Trump again raised the issue of protecting Japan, referring to the fifty thousand American troops based there. He said, "We've got our soldiers sitting there watching (North Korean) missiles go up, and you say to yourself, oh that's interesting. Now we're protecting Japan because Japan is a natural location for North Korea. So we're protecting them and you say to yourself, 'Well, what we are getting out of this?'"

Trump was apparently unaware that Japan is the largest foreign contributor to U.S. missile defense. Japanese destroyers armed with anti-missile missiles patrol side by side with U.S. ships in the waters off North Korea, and Japan is prepared to shoot down any missile headed to Japan *or* the United States. Every Japanese destroyer armed with anti-missile missiles is one less American destroyer that must be deployed.

Japanese confusion over Trump's misunderstanding of the relationship and the responsibilities the two countries share was the principle reason that new defense secretary James Mattis's first overseas trip was to Japan and South Korea.

In a Tokyo news conference in the opening weeks of the administration, he described Japan as "a model of cost sharing and burden sharing." He praised Japanese prime minister Abe for increasing defense spending. He assured the Japanese privately and repeatedly in public that the United States would honor its treaty obligation to come to Japan's defense if it should be attacked.

"I want there to be no misunderstanding. We stand firmly, 100 percent, shoulder to shoulder with you and the Japanese people," he told Abe as they sat down to talk.

It was during the same interview that Sanger and Haberman asked Trump if NATO treaty partners could count on U.S. support if they were attacked by Russia.

"If they fulfill their obligations to us, the answer is yes," he said. As it was in Asia, America's allies were left dumbfounded.

The interviews were just part of the *Times* reporting in 2016 that proved invaluable in understanding the man who would be president. Sanger was also part of a team with Eric Lipton and Scott Shane who pieced together the incredible seven-thousand-word behind-the-scenes story of how Russian spies hacked into the Democratic National Committee files. Another team, David Barstow, Susanne Craig, Russ Buettner and Megan Twohey produced a fascinating report suggesting that Trump had paid no income tax for two decades.

If those were some of the high points, *Times* Executive Editor Dean Baquet told Norah O'Donnell and Gayle King on *CBS This Morning* that he believes the *Times* never got a "handle" on the anger in the heartland of the country.

Interestingly, earlier he had told the *Times* Public Editor Liz Spayd that one reason for that is the decline of local newspapers. With the most powerful news organizations in America in New York and Washington, he said, "That means that whole parts of the country don't get the best coverage that would help us understand the rest of the country."

In March 2017, the Times Company took out a full-page ad in its own newspaper urging readers to subscribe to their local newspaper.

Bumiller and her team in the Washington Bureau learned one thing during the campaign: you never know what's going to happen next, but they can take real pride in this—if the purpose of journalism is to collect independently gathered information that citizens can compare with the government's version of events, the *Times* is upholding its part of the bargain.

Chapter 10

———————————O———————————

The *Wall Street Journal*
Separating Church and State

ONE OF MY FAVORITE STORIES from the Nixon era was when John Ehrlichman, one of Nixon's top aides, called in Arthur Taylor, who at that time was president of the CBS Corporation.

Taylor told me that Ehrlichman asked why he did not call in reporters and tell them to tone down their criticism of Nixon's team.

"I told him there was one simple reason: if I told them to do that they would report it," Taylor said.

When I've repeated the story over the years, some have argued that one would not do that because they would be fired.

Maybe so, I responded, but they would certainly leak it to another news organization. You can't keep that kind of thing secret.

I thought about that when a group of *Wall Street Journal* reporters asked for a meeting with their editor, Gerard Baker, because they reportedly felt the *Journal*'s owners, the Murdoch family, wanted them to go easier on Donald Trump. The reporters didn't just want a meeting; they made sure that was known outside the paper.

The story got my attention because if there is one thing the *Journal* has been known for, especially to other journalists, is the pride its reporters have always taken in separating the news pages from the opinion and editorial pages. Long before Donald Trump's fascination with walls, the *Journal*'s people have proudly called it a wall between church and state.

85

So when he agreed to do our podcast, the wall was what I wanted to talk about with Gerald Seib, the *Journal*'s former Washington Bureau chief, columnist, and *Journal* reporter for thirty-four years.

He confirmed that some reporters were uneasy but wanted to assure me there has been no breach in the wall.

"What's changed," he told me, "is the arrival of Donald Trump, who has changed all the rules, made everybody question the way we do things in politics, in journalism, and out in the country. Our people are trying to figure out how do we handle this guy and people are coming down on different sides of that question, and it's been subject of some debate in our newsroom."

Seib argues that has nothing to do with the ownership. Dow Jones, whose chairman is Rupert Murdoch and who also owns Fox News, owns the *Journal*.

There is no question the *Journal*'s opinion pages are the cornerstone of establishment conservatism, but Seib contends that has no more influence on the news pages than it ever did. Nor does he believe Murdoch and his sons want that.

Seib cites the editorial page as the best argument for his belief.

The *Journal*'s editorial page took a hard line against Hillary Clinton to be sure, but Seib says the *Journal*'s editorials "wacked away" at Trump consistently throughout the campaign and have continued into his presidency.

If anything that would prove to be an understatement. In March the *Journal*'s editorial page unleashed one of the harshest attacks to be leveled at Trump throughout the entire campaign and the early days of his presidency, accusing him of "an endless stream of exaggerations, evidence-free accusations, implausible denials and other falsehoods."

The editorial characterized Trump's refusal to take back his allegation that Obama had wiretapped him by declaring: "The President clings to his accusation like a drunk to an empty gin bottle."

The problem, Seib says, is that *Journal* reporters are grappling with the same challenge facing other news organizations: How do you handle it when the president of the United States says things that are simply not true?

"There's been a debate about whether you say he lied about something or whether you say he said something that's not true.

"We've come down on the side of telling the reader, 'this is not accurate,' and let the reader decide if he lied or just doesn't know what he's talking about."

We spoke after a morning tweet by the president claiming that President Obama had released 122 vicious criminals from Guantanamo who returned to the battlefield as terrorists.

"That wasn't true," Seib said. "Most of them were released by George W. Bush. So we wrote the story and said he kept up his attack on former President Obama but misstated a key fact in doing so."

Then the *Journal* gave the actual facts—Obama released nine of the prisoners, Bush released 113.

Two days after our interview with Seib, the *Journal* broke another story sure to displease Trumpland—that Trump's daughter Ivanka and her husband, Jared Kushner, were renting their new Washington home from a Chilean billionaire embroiled in a dispute with the U.S. government over a Minnesota mine worth billions of dollars.

A company controlled by the Chilean, Andronico Luksic, bought the Washington mansion after the November election, and the Kushners moved in around the time of the Inauguration.

The tycoon's family controls a Chilean empire of mining, banking, and industrial interests estimated by *Forbes* magazine to be worth $13.1 billion.

According to the *Journal*, the Obama administration blocked the company from building a giant copper and nickel mine adjacent to a Minnesota wilderness area. Some Minnesota politicians are urging the Trump administration to reverse the decision.

A company spokesman said the Chilean company bought the house as an investment in Washington's Kalorama area not far from where former President Obama is living. He said the rental to the Kushners was coincidental and had no relationship to the company's dispute with the U.S. government. He said the couple was paying "absolute market value" in rent.

A White House spokeswoman said the couple had looked at the house late last year and told a broker they had no interest in buying it but wanted to rent it. The spokeswoman said the real estate broker knew of a potential buyer and "put the deal together."

Like the *Times* and *Post*, the *Journal* is beefing up White House coverage; where three reporters once covered the White House now there will be six. Like the *Times*, one reporter will be on early tweet patrol.

"We have basically turned our thinking upside down," Seib told me. "We used to have one deadline a day late in the afternoon; now there's a deadline of one kind or another every hour."

Early in the administration I asked him how long he expected the chaotic pace to continue.

"Over time things usually revert to the norm," he said. "I tell people things calm down (when) people new to government figure out that the way things were done were done for a reason and so they return to normal."

But not this time, he says, "because Donald Trump is proudly not a normal politician."

While Seib believes news organizations—at least the big ones—are positioning themselves to survive the new communications environment, he's not so sure about the political parties.

He believes the entire electoral process is in turmoil, and both political parties are in the midst of an identity crisis.

He says Republicans nominated a populist who is not really a traditional conservative and not all that friendly to some of the business community's desires.

Nor, he said, was Trump's message in line with the usual Republican rhetoric.

"He went to the Conservative Political Action Conference and said from now on the Republican Party will be the party of the worker," he said.

As for the Democrats, he noted that most of the populist energy on that side of the spectrum was identified with Bernie Sanders, a proud Independent Socialist. So he wonders, what does it mean to be a Democrat or Republican? More specifically, what does it mean to be a Democratic or Republican populist?

"Compare all this to the '90s when Bill Clinton and his Third Way represented a middle-of-the-road Democratic Party and there was a fairly middle-of-the-road Conservative Bush Republican Party," Seib said. "We've moved to new ground in both parties."

His theory is that 2016 came down to Hillary Clinton and Trump because she was able to overcome the party's populist impulses and hang on as the representative of the Democratic establishment, but what had not been anticipated was that she had hung on by her fingernails—no one in politics anticipated the strong challenge Sanders would present.

"What if Biden—a kind of working man's Democrat, had run? Maybe it would have been his year," he said.

Seib believes Trump won because he did figure out the populist uprising or just happened to walk through the door at the precise moment when being the establishment figure was no longer the ticket to success for the Republican Party. He believes it could have been someone else, but it happened to Trump. Pertinent to his argument, the last Republicans left standing in 2016 were the two who were least friendly to the Republican establishment—Ted Cruz and Trump.

If you gave Democrats truth serum, he believes they would tell you that if they could do it over, they would have picked someone other than Clinton.

"Because it turns out, being the very embodiment of the political establishment was the worst possible profile for 2014.

"Trump got one thing through to people during the campaign and that was he could be the agent of change," he said.

If there is one thing to be said for Campaign 2016, it was a learning experience for all of us—politicians and the press.

As for journalism at the *Wall Street Journal*, I found it still healthy and thriving. It was always a good newspaper, and somewhat to my surprise, I concluded in recent years that it became a better general-interest newspaper under the Murdochs. If they were pressuring their reporters to go easier on Trump, they, too, learned another important lesson in 2016—their reporters will make sure the rest of us know about it.

Chapter 11

⸻⸺○⸺⸻

The *Texas Tribune*
Filling a Texas-Size Void

FEW NEWSPAPERS HAVE HAD THE ECONOMIC MEANS (and sometimes the foresight) to reorganize themselves in the ways the *Washington Post*, the *New York Times*, and to some extent, the *Wall Street Journal* have done. The decline of newspapers in Texas, a state of twenty-seven million people, has been especially hard hit by newspaper closures and cutbacks.

That's why we wanted to talk with Evan Smith who founded the *Texas Tribune* to fill the void.

Smith has never been one to walk away from a challenge. As we used to say when I was growing up in Fort Worth, he was eating high on the hog in 2009. He was the hugely successful editor of *Texas Monthly*, the critically acclaimed, financially successful magazine whose circulation and influence reached far beyond Texas. In campaign years, his Austin office was the obligatory first stop for visiting political reporters from across the United States.

But he walked away from all of that and embarked on a mission that, in truth, left even some of his friends wondering exactly what he had in mind. With partners he founded something called the *Texas Tribune*, a news-gathering organization whose stated purpose was to gather news about politics and state government then give it away—to whoever wanted it.

Say what?

You heard right. Give it away. As in free. This, in a state that had seen journalists becoming an endangered species as newspaper after newspaper went broke and news coverage, especially political news coverage, had all but dried up. Smith's idea was that his team would do the reporting and Texans could have whatever news they found free of charge.

It worked. Entering its eighth year, the *Tribune* is a highly viable, online, nonprofit, nonpartisan organization that has become arguably the most influential political news outlet in the state. It employs dozens of reporters, by far the largest staff of political journalists in the state, and much of the year, *Tribune* reporters make up nearly half the reporters in the state capital.

How has he done it? First, through fact-based reporting and deft financing. In eight years, Smith and his team have raised $41 million through conferences, special events, and in donations from individuals, foundations, and corporations.

"We're a nonprofit 501c3 organization that we believe exists in the public interest," he told us. "We think we are improving the life of the community. We didn't think we could exist as a for-profit business. If you could make a profit off this, the for-profit guys wouldn't have cut back coverage right? Think of us as NPR or PBS, more than as a traditional charity."

Some of the money comes from national foundations like Gates, Knight, and Ford, but some comes from the Texas rich (the state has no shortage in millionaires and billionaires).

"We also get a lot of gifts from regular folks who send us ten or fifty or a hundred bucks," he says.

There is no question the *Texas Tribune* is filling a need. When I left Fort Worth in 1969 to work for CBS News in Washington, nearly all metropolitan newspapers in the state were home owned (the *Dallas Morning News* was owned by A. H. Belo Corporation, but it was based in Dallas). Belo still owns the *Morning News*, but the rest—the ones that have survived—are all owned by out-of-state companies, and some are but a shell of what they once were.

Smith says his purpose was not to replace the state's existing newspapers but simply augment what they were doing.

Over the past thirty years, the *Fort Worth Press*, the *Dallas Times Herald*, the *San Antonio Light*, and the *Houston Post* have closed, and most newspapers have reduced staff severely.

Smith noted that the *Fort Worth Star-Telegram* (my old paper) no longer even maintains a bureau in the state capital.

"Think about that," he says. "Fort Worth is the sixteenth largest city in the country. It's one of six cities in Texas in the nation's top twenty most populated cities, and they have absolutely no coverage in the state capital." (Reporters from the home office do report from Austin from time to time.)

Fort Worth is not alone. Smith says the number of reporters covering the state government is about a third of what it was twenty years ago in a state that will be home to fifty-four million people by 2050.

So, yes, he says, the *Tribune* is there to fill that void.

"We have a lot of reporters and we can do a lot, we can't do everything but we try to make our content available to as many people as we can," he told us. "The Texas legislature meets only every other year, and once it adjourns many of the papers that still send a reporter to Austin bring them home."

Smith's people are there year round and they do not cover sports and other beats, so their reporters have time to keep eyes and ears on every state agency and official.

Smith says that when the *Tribune* began in 2009, there were five million paid newspaper readers in Texas. Two and a half million lived in the big cities—Austin, Dallas, Fort Worth, Houston, and San Antonio.

"Those were the only cities that had reporters covering the state capital," he said. Currently, the El Paso paper has stationed a reporter in Austin, and the combined paper in Amarillo and Lubbock stationed a reporter at the capital for a time. But outside Dallas, Houston, Austin, and San Antonio, the rest of the state must rely on the Associated Press, and the wire service does not localize its coverage for specific markets.

"So we give our stuff away," Smith said. "The people who don't live in the big towns are no less Texans than we are, and have no access to information about what their state government is doing."

Smith sees a direct correlation between Texas's traditionally low voter turnout and the lack of political news coverage.

"I can draw a dotted line from the cutback of political news coverage over the last ten to fifteen years to the fact that we have the worst voter turnout in the nation," he said.

The numbers are startling. In 2010, Texas was fifty-first out of fifty (it lagged behind the District of Columbia as well as the fifty states).

"As I understand the numbers, we got to forty-six in 2016 but overall for the last four election cycles we were last in the nation," he said.

Smith blames the media for part of that. He's says it is the responsibility of journalists to "tee up for busy people the things that are important enough for them to pay attention to, whether it's their family lives that are keeping them from paying attention or their work lives."

"The media's job is to say, stop, this is important!" he told us.

"When you have fewer reporters and fewer papers and not much of an appetite for covering this stuff . . . because it's not particularly sexy, then the media has not done its job.

"I think that is absolutely why in a state with paltry coverage there is also paltry interest among readers."

Smith says, "If you want to distill the *Texas Tribune* mission it is this: 'A smarter Texas is a better Texas, however you define smarter, however you define better.'"

The *Tribune* does not take editorial stands. Having an editorial page leads to charges of bias, he believes, even when opinion does not bleed into straight news stories because readers tend to conflate opinion pages with the straight news section. So, he leaves editorial stands to the existing newspapers.

"Being nonpartisan allows us to say we don't care what choices people make specifically but we do care that they make choices," he said.

Because the media, too many times, has not been able to alert the public to things that matter, he adds, civic participation has fallen.

Even so, Smith believes the most significant reason voter turnout in Texas has fallen is the gerrymandering of congressional and state voting districts.

He calls it the "greatest cancer on democracy," which has led to profoundly noncompetitive elections in Texas and across the nation. Once Texas primary elections are held, he says he can predict accurately all but four or five of the more than three hundred elections across the state for Congress, the state legislature, and other statewide office holders.

Through trade-offs and deals among officeholders, voting districts have become incumbent protection societies. District lines are so narrowly drawn they can sometimes snake from cities like Fort Worth in North Texas to South Texas counties hundreds of miles away on the Texas coast. Once elected, an incumbent can raise money to stave off challengers for years.

People see it as rigged, conclude their vote means nothing, and see no reason to go to the polls, he argues.

Unlike many national pollsters, politicians, and journalists, Smith does not believe the growth of the Hispanic population in Texas means the blue Republican state will become a neutral battleground state or possibly Democratic anytime soon.

Once a Democratic bastion, Texas did not elect a Republican to statewide office until 1960 when John Tower won a special election to fill the Senate seat vacated by Lyndon Johnson when he became John Kennedy's running mate. In 1976, Jimmy Carter became the last Democratic presidential candidate to carry Texas. Today all statewide officeholders are Republican, and the legislature is heavily Republican.

Smith says it will take more than a big turnout of Hispanics who normally vote Democratic to put Democrats back in control. He says the way the state is changing should make it an easy pick off for Democrats, but he says the Democrats just don't have their act together—they don't have candidates and they don't have a party infrastructure to win.

He points to recent elections: In 2008, Barack Obama beat John McCain by seventeen thousand votes in Harris County, home of Houston, Texas's largest city, which has a large minority population. But as his popularity faded in 2012, he beat Mitt Romney there by fewer than one thousand votes. Hillary Clinton, on the other hand, carried Harris County by 160,000 votes in 2016 even though she lost the state by nine points. In fact, Clinton won all of the big urban areas with the exception of Fort Worth-Tarrant County.

"What Democrats needed to do was not just turn out people of color in those urban areas, they also needed to turn out white Democrats. Democrats here lost whites the way they did in the Midwest and other places. Unless white Democrats turn out, the Hispanics will not be able to carry them to victory," he said.

For all the criticism and concern and attacks on the media, Smith said that many news organizations did remarkable and valuable work in 2016 that should be celebrated.

Among those whose work he considered exceptionable is *Washington Post* reporter David Fahrenthold, whose investigation of Donald Trump's charities produced multiple eyebrow-raising disclosures.

"I have a picure of David Fahrenthold in my house," he said, "the way many Texans have a picture of the Virgin of Guadalupe."

Chapter 12

———————○———————

Island in the Stream
CBS News Goes Digital

BY THE TIME THE 2016 CAMPAIGN got underway, all of the network and cable channels were adding more platforms—websites, podcasts, and newsletters. As the new administration was taking shape, NBC lured Fox News anchor Megyn Kelly to its stable of correspondents and expanded its overseas reach by buying a stake in a European news-gathering network. But CBS took the most radical step in 2014 when it launched a 24/7 all-news digital outlet aimed at phones and other mobile devices.

It all started in 2012. The CBS Corporation was offered a chance to bid on buying Current TV, the cable channel owned by former Vice President Al Gore and his partners. The CBS team thought it was worth about $125 to $150 million.

It later sold to the Arab kingdom of Qatar for $500 million and became Al-Jazeera America, an ill-fated venture that never caught on and shut down in mid-2016.

At the time, thirty-nine-year-old David Rhodes, the newly installed president of CBS News, had argued against buying the channel.

Instead, he said CBS should adapt a "cable bypass strategy." CBS had not been involved with cable since 1981 when founder William S. Paley created a channel devoted to the arts and culture. The channel was critically acclaimed but never found an audience and shut down in fourteen months.

Rhodes believed buying back into cable where CBS would be starting out behind CNN, Fox, and MSNBC was just bad strategy. One analogy he used was that CBS should be like a developing country that had no landline phones. It wouldn't build a landline phone infrastructure; it would go straight to mobile. He argued CBS should skip cable technology and go straight to streaming, where Netflix and Amazon were already introducing audiences to entertainment programming.

CBS began a search for distribution streaming partners and discussed the idea with several companies, including YouTube. In the end, CBS Interactive Chief Jim Lanzone convinced the Corporation that CBS could create a streaming channel in house. The decision to go forward was not unanimous, but the in-house distribution made the difference and gave CBS the ability to do it at low enough cost to take the risk.

So it was that in November 2014, just two years after Al Gore's Current Channel was auctioned off to Qatar, CBSN debuted. Al Gore may not have created the Internet as he seemed to suggest in the 2000 campaign, but the sale of his cable channel was clearly the catalyst that started Rhodes and his CBS colleagues thinking about the world of streaming.

When Rhodes called streaming "the future of news" in March 2016, some remained dubious. But by the end of the year, many in the industry conceded that Rhodes and CBSN were on to something.

Audience measurements in 2015 showed that CBSN had attracted 74.2 million streams—that is, 74.2 million viewers had tuned in to the channel, either to watch live or to download something from its archive of speeches, statements, or other newsworthy events. But during the election year that had increased to a whopping 207 percent to 227.9 million streams.

On election night, CBS simulcast its network coverage on the digital network and recorded a record 19.1 million streams on CBSN. That included 11.1 unique visitors, people who tuned in more than once.

The evening's best news was that those who watched the digital network often stayed tuned for forty minutes. Viewers split three ways: about a third watched on desktop computers, a third watched through streaming devices on their televisions such as Roku, and a third watched on phones, a pattern that has remained consistent since CBSN began transmitting.

Currently, CBSN offers a mix of breaking news, original reporting, rebroadcasts of stories seen on the network broadcast news programs, plus the archive of significant speeches, statements, and news events.

Rhodes is convinced that what makes it work is that it meets the expectations of what longtime viewers have come to expect of CBS.

"It is CBS News, the same editorial standards and the same people you see on our other broadcasts," he told me. "That's where we start."

Rhodes is aware that by 2020, two-thirds of online activity will be on phones, and many younger people are already getting most of their news from their mobile devices. He wants younger viewers, but CBSN is not aimed at just the young.

He told me what he tells others: "The audience this is designed for is an audience that is interested in news."

To Rhodes, the great changes of the digital age are the overriding constant in communication.

During our podcast, he told us, "I don't think (journalism) is being remade, it's evolving. The thing about media and news is you're always going through a technology transition. This company navigated a very successful transition from radio to television while maintaining a robust radio operation.

"So if you've accomplished a transition from no pictures to all moving pictures, I think you can get through a lot.

"This is one that's going to reset things as much as that one reset things, but it's going to leave some people behind—it's like movies going from silent to talkies."

While CBS News is devoting much of its attention to digital, Rhodes emphasizes it is adding a platform, not deemphasizing broadcast operations. Like the *Washington Post*, which has expanded from a newspaper company to a media company with multiple outlets, CBS is finding more ways to reach news consumers.

Industry observers have been predicting the demise of the network evening news broadcast since the days when their audiences began to diminish with new competition from cable. But

Rhodes says he has no intention of phasing out the CBS Evening News.

"As long as five, six or seven million people show up to watch it," he says, "we're going to present it."

He concedes that the network's morning broadcast has received parity with the evening program, and though its audience is not as large as evening news audiences, it continues to attract new viewers. Because of the hour it airs, it may be the only time period when viewers tune in unaware of the headlines.

Rhodes takes seriously the criticism of the media in the 2016 campaign, but he also takes it in stride.

"The media is never blameless, but there's always a blame-the-media phase of any campaign—we just entered the blame-the-media phase a little earlier this time," he said.

He noted that Bernie Sanders accused the media of going easy on Clinton, Clinton's criticism of the media became a thriving cottage industry, and Trump railed about the media at his rallies and in countless tweets.

The blame-the-media phase generally tends to come when large groups don't like a particular outcome and don't really believe it could have been arrived at fairly.

On Trump, Rhodes says the criticism broke into three narratives: "you the media created Trump; you were taken in by the entertainment so basically you enabled this over the will of the people—it was good for ratings so you went with it.

"Second, you missed Trump. The media are elitist. They didn't see Trump coming and they missed the story. They thought it was going to be someone else.

"And the third narrative is that the media really didn't matter. What's been elemental to Trump's success and popularity has been his use of Twitter and social media to essentially go around the independent media.

"Well, choose your own adventure here. It can't be all of the above," he said.

Like most of us in journalism, Rhodes worries about the impact of so many failing local newspapers, but he wonders if streaming technology may provide the alternative. He remembers when Chicago's City News Service had stringers or reporters in every police precinct and fed stories to Chicago's newspapers.

What CBSN is trying to do at the national level may well prove economically feasible at the local level, he says.

Successful journalism at the local and national level, in Rhodes's opinion, must be grounded in accurate, relevant information delivered to news consumers in timely fashion in language they can understand.

"I'm a New Yorker," he told me. "I grew up here, this is my hometown and I have this theory that everybody here is in the information business, we don't make anything here. This is not a place where we make energy like Houston, or cars like Detroit. We move information around.

"So whether people are in the news media where the information is about what we've been talking about, or in finance where I might have information about the pricing of some asset, I'm going to try and sell that information to you or maybe even in fashion and you want to know what's going to be 'hot' next year, 'take a seat on the runway and I'm going to show you,' these are all basically information businesses.

"In the end that's what journalism is all about—if I have a piece of information that you want to know, I'll figure out a way to get a rent for that. But, I have to have the information, don't I?

"I have to know something that you might want to know. Otherwise this all falls apart."

That's how American journalism became a viable industry as it gave its citizens the information they needed to make democracy work.

Rhodes says CBS News became what it is with original reporting by talented journalists, and the mission will never change. But with CBSN, he says, it has a new tool to carry it out.

Chapter 13

———○———

Andy Lack
Around the World and Back for More

WHEN YOU'RE TRYING TO FIGURE OUT what's ahead, it never hurts to take a look back every so often. That's why I sought out Andrew Lack.

Andy Lack reminds me of that insurance company commercial that goes, "we know a lot because we've seen a lot." That's Andy; he's been around the block a time or two—around the world actually, and he's learned a thing or two. These days he's in his second time around running NBC News.

Don't worry that he is any way bored with the job. He's like a rookie reporter who's been sent out on his first story.

"I hesitate to say this because people may misunderstand," he told me. "If you're in our line of work it's exciting as hell to come to work every day."

It's not as if he's had a dull life. I first knew him in the 1980s when he was the *60 Minutes* producer who snuck into Afghanistan with Dan Rather to report from the battlefield as Afghan irregulars fought Russian troops. The hair-raising stories earned Rather the nickname "Gunga Dan." During his years at CBS News, Lack won an astounding sixteen Emmys and four DuPont awards. Between CBS News and his first stop at NBC in 1993, Lack was CEO of Bloomberg's Global Media Group and later CEO of Sony Music. He returned to NBC News after the Brian Williams fiasco, righted the ship, and plunged into coverage of the

2016 campaign, which he calls an episode unparalleled in his thirty-five-year career.

Without passing judgment on the rightness or wrongness of the actions, Lack admits he was impressed at the way Trump had managed to do a lot of what he promised in the campaign during his first week in office.

The actions came with considerable commotion and provoked demonstrations and a series of nasty attacks on the press. When I asked him how he was directing his reporters to react, he said he simply told them "to stay cool."

"We've seen it before," he said. "Trump's attitude toward the press is not unfamiliar ground. We were hearing about Trump's Monday night massacre [when he fired Acting Attorney General Sally Yates for refusing to enforce his proposed travel ban], which was a reminder of Nixon's Saturday Night Massacre when he fired the special prosecutor investigating Watergate and then Attorney General Elliott Richardson and his deputy William Ruckelshaus resigned.

"This presidency is going to be a test of our character, a test of character for many news organizations," Lack said.

"Trump's senior advisor Bannon told us to shut up and said we were the opposition party," Lack said. "We are not the opposition party, we are an independent group of fellows, a diverse group, and we pride ourselves on our independence—we are journalists. That doesn't comport well with this White House.

"As Tom Brokaw said, 'We just have to be immune to the contentiousness, the hostility, to challenges that the Trump administration is throwing at us in terms of their feelings about us.'"

I asked Lack if he thought it was all just a new president blowing off steam, or was it a strategy.

"I do think it runs deep, and I do think it is a strategy," he said. "Look, there is great skepticism about the media among ordinary Americans from all walks and there always has been.

"We have experienced it over the years at NBC, but we haven't been called out the way this administration has done it. But that's the territory were in, and we've got to understand that and not be pushed back by it but acknowledge it and deal with it."

Lack acknowledges there is considerable skepticism about the media. A Gallup poll taken as Trump took office showed only 32 percent of those questioned had only a "fair to great deal of trust" in the press. Lack believes some of that is part of the growing distrust of all institutions, but some of it, he feels, is simply endemic to the press and what it does.

"We've never been in a popularity contest. We don't win those nor should we. That's not our role," he said.

Lack's answer reminded me of an experience I had long ago at a CBS affiliates convention during the Walter Cronkite era. All the correspondents got a nice round of applause as we were individually introduced, but when Charles Kuralt rose the applause was so deafening that Kuralt himself was embarrassed. While the rest of us were covering politics and wars and other untoward events, Kuralt traveled the American backroads doing heartwarming stories about average Americans who did extraordinary things.

When the rest of us ribbed him about the applause he got, Kuralt said, "Remember boys, sometimes you have to tell people news they don't want to hear. All my stories have happy endings."

The truth is none of us like to get bad news, even when we need to know it, and sometimes our viewers tend to blame the messenger. By definition most of the news we deliver is probably bad. As Walter Cronkite used to say, "The cat that stays home is not news, the cat that runs away is what the neighborhood talks about."

As Walter also used to say, "and that's the way it is," but the rise of so-called fake news has complicated the situation for everyone.

"I'm not distressed about people's attitude toward us generally. But I think we get uncomfortable because journalism is now represented online by lots of very bad actors," Lack adds.

"We work very hard to be as transparent and honest and clear as we can possibly be," he says. But he admits it's a little uncomfortable to be thrown into the same basket with some of the Internet's bad actors who have different values and little regard for truth.

"Fake news has taken on new meaning in a digital world. It is a serious issue for us . . . and an assault on all of us whether you're a journalist or whatever line of work you're in."

Lack worries that the partisan divide in the country has created filters that many people employ to get their news—conservatives going to one source, liberals to another.

"If you are getting your news from only one source, I would respectfully submit you're not getting a good look at what's going on in the country," he said.

Lack believes reporters must seek out not just how Washington reacts to the actions of the new administration but how it is going down in the rest of the country.

"We've got our work cut out for us," he says. But as difficult and challenging as he expects it to be, you get the feeling Lack is almost jealous of his young reporters who will be manning the front lines.

"Hallie Jackson, Katy Tur, Kasie Hunt, the gang I like to call our road warriors, they really came of age in terms of covering the 2016 campaign. Imagine that for a second! Your first campaign! It was a new world for reporters to have all those tools to distribute the information that they were getting, not just with their own news organization but on these social media platforms, Snapchat, Twitter, Facebook—tools that didn't exist even ten years ago.

"That phone in my hand has changed my life," he says. "We're going to have a civics lesson that challenges us every day, challenges us with questions about our courts, about the executive branch, the Congress in ways that if I were twenty-five and at NBC News I'd be saying I can't be luckier than this.

"But that is for the work. For how you feel personally or the challenges for the country—that's separate, that's a separate matter."

That zeal for the work and the ability to separate it from personal feelings is what drives journalism. It is also the hardest part for those outside the profession to understand.

Chapter 14

———————O———————

The Cable Guy(s)

IN THE CLOSING DAYS of the 2016 campaign, the joke around newsrooms was faux regret that Charles Dickens had already used the line "it was the best of times, it was the worst of times." It would have been the perfect title for the story of Fox News in 2016.

On the plus side, Fox had its highest ratings ever—not just ahead of its cable news competitors, CNN and MSNBC, but as Fox News anchor Chris Wallace proudly noted, "The highest in cable period, that means we also beat ESPN and TNT . . . entertainment, sports, and news and that feels good."

In addition, Wallace was the first Fox reporter chosen to moderate a presidential debate, an assignment that produced very good reviews.

Fox News employees were told it was their best year financially since 2003, and it was the first time ever that Fox finished the year with the largest number of viewers in both daytime and prime time.

But there was also plenty on the debit side of the ledger. Roger Ailes, the founder and shaper of Fox News, was ousted in a nasty sexual harassment scandal that cost the company $20 million to settle, according to multiple sources, and after a dispute with Fox brass, Megyn Kelly, anchor of Fox's second highest rated prime-time program, slipped away to NBC, to be followed shortly by Greta Van Susteren, another popular Fox anchor.

But that turmoil was only prelude to the departure of Bill O'Reilly in April 2017 after the *New York Times* reported that sexual harassment suits filed against O'Reilly had cost Fox and O'Reilly $13 million. O'Reilly was without question Fox's biggest star, and his program reportedly took in more than $400 million a year in advertising. Throughout the controversy, O'Reilly maintained his innocence, but with Ailes gone he had lost his main defender, and the Murdock family that controls Fox decided the time had come to part company with O'Reilly as well as Ailes.

Within weeks of O'Reilly's departure, there was another shock. On May 18, Ailes suffered a fall at his Florida home and died. O'Reilly, meanwhile was being offered new platforms by other conservative outlets.

The "best of times, worst of times" analogy was apt to describe Fox News, but it could be applied as well to the entire cable universe. Sports giant ESPN, Turner Broadcasting, and Univision saw significant drops in their audiences as they became victims of so-called cord cutting—the growing practice of TV viewers to discontinue the costly fees required to bring cable programming into their homes.

The "best of times" for cable was pretty much confined to cable news outlets and not just Fox.

After some bad years, CNN had one of its best years ever, as it pulled closer to Fox and increased the number of younger viewers sought by advertisers. Under the guidance of Andrew Lack, who returned to NBC after the Brian Williams fiasco, even MSNBC, the lowest rated of three cable services, had its best year since the Tim Russert era. In fact, it registered the largest percentage gain of new viewers of all the cable outlets.

But the warning flags for cable as well as the networks cannot be ignored. The trend of younger viewers to turn to other sources for news is obvious in the ratings: the median viewer age for Fox is sixty-six, sixty-three for MSNBC, and sixty-one for CNN. The challenge for all of them is the same one faced by all news organizations: In calmer times, can they still maintain viewers at a level that will ensure economic viability necessary to pay for aggressive and comprehensive news coverage?

For all the questions, cable played an enormously influential role in the 2016 campaigns; the broadcast networks brought big audiences on the nights they took the airways; their Sunday shows still produced next-day headlines; newspapers, especially the *Times* and *Post*, got the biggest scoops and had the space to print them; and younger Americans got much of their political news from social media, especially Facebook, but because they were always there 24/7, the cable shows often drove political coverage.

I've never been one to believe you can give people too much coverage; our job as political journalists is to tell people as much as we know, and the voters can take it or leave it as they see best. Nevertheless, the cable companies' nonstop coverage irritated many. CNN became a favorite whipping boy of the Trump campaign while anti-Trump people argued the nonstop coverage was responsible for Trump's surprise victory.

Perhaps surprisingly, I discovered two of cable's most respected reporters, Fox Sunday show moderator Chris Wallace and CNN anchor Jake Tapper, agreed with their critics—they had given Trump too much airtime.

When I asked Wallace if Fox gave Trump too much exposure, he said, "Absolutely! I thought frankly that CNN was worse than we were but we were plenty bad at Fox where we would have the camera on the empty podium and say 'waiting for Trump rally.' People said we made Trump; no, we didn't make Trump, Trump was a phenomenon and we were chasing the ratings of Trump . . . we were following the crowd, not leading the crowd. But you know that was unfair. We shouldn't have given him that kind of coverage."

When I asked Tapper about it in a separate interview, he agreed, saying, "Especially in 2015 when he announced—and the Trump phenomenon started to happen—and he was filling those arenas with thousands and thousands of people and the other candidates were not, I think it's true and (CNN president) Jeff Zucker acknowledged as much, that CNN ran too many of those rallies unedited, start to finish without fact checking, etc. I think it's true, and I think MSNBC and Fox did the same thing."

Wallace is proud of one thing. He decided in the beginning that he would not put Trump on his Sunday show by phone, a decision he admits came at a price.

"I'd never seen a candidate doing phoners on a Sunday show where the emphasis is supposed to be in-depth interviews, not breaking news. We were the only ones who said it and we took a hit because we did—even on the phone he got better ratings," he said. (As we noted earlier, Wallace also got far fewer interviews with Trump than the other Sunday broadcasts.)

Providing balanced coverage is not always as easy as it might seem, and Tapper reminded me of that when he told me about trying to book his debut Sunday show in June 2015. He extended invitations to Hillary Clinton, Jeb Bush, and Marco Rubio. Tapper wanted to make a big splash so he offered each of them—one at a time—the entire hour.

"I told them, we'll tell your life story," he said. "To Jeb Bush I said, you can tell us how you met your wife, I told Clinton's people we'll ask her about her work with the Children's Defense Fund, I told Rubio I'd ask him about his parents coming from Cuba. Yes, I told them, there will be some adversarial moments, but I'll give you the whole hour.'"

And they all turned him down because, he said, they all thought the "old formula worked"—that is, control the narrative; never put your candidate in the position of having to answer questions to which they may not know the answer; and do Sunday shows only now and then, mainly from a remote location and only when you have news to announce in seven-minute spurts.

"It was like pulling teeth to get them on television," he said. "Donald Trump would do it all the time. And he would take tough questions all the time and then he would come back. . . . I think that helped him, I think his willingness to get in the mix and engage helped him."

Booking Sunday shows is a book unto itself, but as one who spent twenty-four years doing it, I can assure you that Tapper and Wallace's Sunday colleagues John Dickerson, George Stephanopoulous, and Chuck Todd would readily agree.

Like all news organizations, the cable companies constantly deal with charges of bias and how they are perceived by the public. Wallace says Fox News was created two decades ago to provide an alternative to the broadcast networks that Fox creators considered "left leaning." "Whether or not the networks were leaning left, Fox News has been extremely successful and has become the go-to channel for conservatives, especially Trump fans."

What Fox was to Trump's folk in 2016, MSNBC was where Hillary Clinton supporters found empathy. CNN was often in the middle, under fire from first one side, then the other, depending on whose ox was being gored on a particular day.

Wallace understands the criticism and says there is no question Fox takes a view from the right in prime time, but he argues there is something of a firewall during the day. He points out that unlike MSNBC, Fox does not use its pundits such as Bill O'Reilly and Sean Hannity to anchor special events such as election nights when he, Bret Baier, and Brit Hume have often led the coverage. Prime time is Fox's op-ed page, he says. Unlike most op-ed pages, it makes the money that keeps the whole operation running.

When I asked NBC News Chief Andrew Lack about MSNBC's liberal reputation, he readily conceded that was accurate, but since returning to NBC in 2015, he has been moving to put more emphasis during the day on straight, solid news coverage. He also pointed out to me that MSNBC's most popular pundit is Joe Scarborough, a one-time conservative Republican congressman from Florida.

Scarborough carved out a unique role for himself during the 2016 campaign. Trump watches the show religiously and often calls in without invitation, but while Scarborough took the calls and gave Trump extended airtime, he was also one of Trump's strongest critics. One memorable morning, he hung up on Trump as Trump went off on a rampage.

Early in his presidency when Trump attacked the federal judge who had temporarily overturned his immigration ban, Scarborough wrote an op-ed in the *Washington Post* saying Trump's reaction was unacceptable. "As the White House improves its internal decision making process, West Wing staffers would do the country and world a great service if they could somehow apply a similar discipline to the president's Twitter feed."

For whatever reasons, Trump always seems to come back for more.

Jeff Zucker, the one-time boy wonder of NBC News who became executive producer of the *Today Show* while in his twenties, took over CNN in 2012 and has guided its resurgence. He doesn't give many interviews about his job and politely declined our request saying he preferred to let CNN's work speak for itself.

The work in 2016 held up well. In the last days of Trump's transition, Tapper and a team that included National Security correspondent Jim Sciutto, Justice Department correspondents Evan Perez and Pamela Brown, and one-time Watergate reporter Carl Bernstein broke a huge story.

In carefully worded detail, they told how America's top Intelligence officials had given Trump a briefing on Russia hacking in an attempt to meddle in our electoral process. Included in the briefing was an unsubstantiated document from a non-Intelligence source that claimed the Russians also had information that could be used to blackmail the president.

CNN, as did several news organizations, had obtained the document some weeks earlier but had been unable to confirm any of the allegations and chose not to release it. When they learned that the Intelligence officials considered it important enough to bring to Trump's attention, they decided to include that in their report. Even then, they did not disclose its contents. Within minutes after its release, however, the website BuzzFeed released the entire document, which was filled with salacious allegations involving Trump and Russian prostitutes. BuzzFeed editor Ben Smith said he followed the rule "when in doubt publish" and argued the public had a right to know what the fuss was about.

Tapper has known and liked Smith for years and has been an admirer of his work, but he was stunned that BuzzFeed had made the decision to release the document. To Tapper that was irresponsible. Like most mainstream reporters and editors, he still favors the old-school rule of "when in doubt, leave it out."

He also worried (correctly as it turned out) that Trump would conflate the BuzzFeed report with CNN's report in an effort to undermine the CNN reporting.

"In short order," Tapper said, "I was accused of doing things I never did, of making charges I never made, of providing information I never did."

The story provoked a nasty exchange the following day when Trump refused to take questions from CNN reporter Jim Acosta and set off an angry round of charges and attacks on the media.

Tapper worries more about the long-term implications than the early commotion.

"Bad journalism undermines good journalism," he says. "People lose faith in us. We really need to get our act together in the Trump era because he is so adversarial with the press. We need to make sure that when we go with something it's true, it's accurate, it's on target.

"And our behavior—people need to watch what they tweet, what they say. There is a big trust chasm.

"What BuzzFeed did, that decision they made, hurt us."

Trump used it to put the media on notice.

Within days he was leveling totally unsubstantiated reports that the media was no longer reporting terrorist incidents and declared that all negative polls about him were fake news.

By late spring Trump's relationship with CNN had deteriorated into an all-out Twitter war. After CNN retracted a story about a Trump confidant and three CNN journalists resigned, Trump circulated a doctored video in which he was seen body slamming a person labeled CNN.

Chapter 15

─────────────○─────────────

The Root
Straight Talk and a Little Shade

DONALD GRAHAM, THEN OWNER of the *Washington Post*, and Harvard historian Henry Lewis Gates Jr. founded The Root.com in 2008 as an outlet for African American voices at a time when there were not many.

Since then it has grown into the premier news, opinion, and cultural site for African American "influencers."

When we asked The Root's managing editor, Danielle Belton, what it offers that other sites don't, she didn't hesitate.

"There is really an unbridledness," she told us. "We really let loose in our opinion and how we think and feel about race and culture and politics. It's very unvarnished. It's very unpolished. We say what we feel. And, we embrace what it means to be black."

That is no small thing. Belton grew up during a time when African Americans were very concerned about how they appeared to white people and the wider culture.

"There was this real feeling," she said, "that if you didn't speak the right way or behave the right way you somehow harmed the whole race. It's called respectability politics.

"The Root doesn't believe that . . . we basically believe that we should accept ourselves fully as who we are and be unvarnished in that and unapologetic and that's really what sets The Root apart."

To Belton, access to the web has given African Americans an influence they never had before. She points to the fact that African

115

Americans' heavy use of Twitter has given them a larger voice in actually shaping the news.

"When protests first started around the deaths of both Trayvon Martin and Michael Brown you had this influx of black people on social media calling out CNN, calling out MSNBC saying why aren't you reporting this? And low and behold people like CNN went to Saint Louis, went to Florida and actually covered those stories and they became national news," she said.

She argues that didn't happen in the past, many times because people just didn't know about it. Now they do, in large part because of the heavy use of social media by African Americans.

Belton says there are also subtler ways that African Americans' participation in social media has changed how people talk about things online.

"The slang and idioms and metaphor that come from black culture have popped up in mainstream media, and it has been fascinating to watch," she laughs. "Like watching mainstream media try to figure out how to use the word 'shade' in a headline so they can say 'Donald Trump Shades CNN.'" The word *shade* in slang terms means to trash talk about someone, according to Belton.

"The only reason it exists is that it came out of a black, gay subculture, then rose out of the subculture into mainstream black culture and into social media, and now it's everywhere," she said.

Belton believes the hunger for information has been fueled by the democratization of the web—not just for African Americans but across all cultural and demographic groups.

"You can get your voice out there now," she said. Belton knows that from experience. Before coming to The Root, she started a blog called "The Black Snob," which quickly grew to a readership of two million people.

The web is an outlet for not just writers and reporters but artists and musicians, and if they have the talent, they can change their lives overnight. Belton had been working at small newspapers where few readers saw her work, but once she started her blog, suddenly her work was seen by thousands and then many more, and it turned her life around.

"We live in this amazing time," Belton said, "where it's like I want to see this movie or I want to hear this music or I want to read this news article and it's all just a few clicks away."

When The Root.com started in 2008, Belton says there were plenty of sites that catered to black Americans' interest in music and entertainment and black culture, but not hard news and political opinion.

"It was a time of great transition in this country—the election of Barack Obama—and people were really excited to just talk about these deep-seated issues that have long affected the country—race, gender, identity." Belton said, "And The Root has been a major player in those discussions."

The Root deals with straight news and opinion, and Belton believes it is important to readers to know when it's one or the other.

"There's nothing wrong with opinion," she told us. "But you still need to back it up with facts. You still need to have sources. When you are writing opinion you can't just throw all caution to the wind and just put it out there. That's a danger because there are some people out there who can't distinguish between opinion and fact."

Belton has mixed feelings about news coverage of the Black Lives Matter movement. On the one hand, she believes it has been helpful because it brought to light several systemic issues around race that affect African Americans. On the other hand, she says journalists tend not to pay attention to African American protests unless they turn violent.

"Big, peaceful protests are overlooked, but if someone breaks a window," she says, "and someone turns over a cop car then the cameras show up."

Belton believes Black Lives Matter protests were covered differently than the women's marches that happened across the country after Trump's inauguration.

"People went on and on—'oh it was so peaceful and wonderful' like there had never been a peaceful protest involving people of color," she said. "And there have been hundreds across the country that have been peaceful and that have been massive and they just don't get the same kind of attention."

"I feel like that just has to do with the fact that a lot of newsrooms are still overwhelmingly white."

What was most on her readers' minds when we interviewed her in the early days of the Trump administration?

In a word, Trump. She said the feelings are all over the place— from anger to disillusionment to grieving and disappointment.

"They are basically going through all the stages of grief," she said. "Some have decided to take this moment as a time to resist, a time of action, be proactive, we need to march and we need to protest and we need to call our congresspersons and let them know how we're thinking. Others are curled up in the fetal position completely freaked out, and then there are those who say 'well, we've seen this before and we've had presidents before we didn't like or agree with and so everybody should just calm down.'

"But it's all about Trump now, that's the hot topic."

Where does she see it all going? Like so many in those early weeks, she had no answer to that.

"We're in uncharted territory," she said. "It's the most unusual presidency in modern history."

Chapter 16

───────○───────

The Year of Living Righteously
NPR Gets Back to Basics

MICHAEL ORESKES IS NO STRANGER to running big, far-flung news organizations. He was a reporter, editor, and then Washington Bureau chief at the *New York Times* and later the editor of the Paris-based *International Herald Tribune*. That led to a top job at the Associated Press where he was managing editor of the wire service's daily news feed. In March 2015, he became National Public Radio's top editor, where he oversees a vast array of news-dispensing platforms including NPR's flagship broadcasts *Morning Edition* and *All Things Considered*.

He is old enough to remember the days when thriving newspapers and three powerful television networks parceled out the news, and he is wise enough to recognize those days are gone forever.

However, he's not afraid to be seen as a little old-fashioned on one thing: the need for tried-and-true journalistic values no matter how much the ways we communicate are changing.

The year 2017, he told us, is the year journalism must get back to basics.

"We are under a lot of pressure," he said. "We're under pressure in a broad sense with the digital transition, the business crisis of so many news organizations, and this struggle we are going to be having with this administration, and I think when you are in that kind of situation you really have to go back to your knitting. You have to figure out exactly who you are."

Journalism's first priority, he says, is to provide reliable, authentic information to the public so they can be who they need to be—good citizens.

"It's really important for us to understand that is our role," he said. "Ultimately, we provide the information that keeps society moving. We have to be really good at it, and we have to recognize our credibility hasn't been that great. We have to rebuild it."

He says that Donald Trump's relentless attacks on reporters and news organizations haven't helped.

"We had a president who came to office attacking the key institutions of the society—both the government and us, the press. And that is a bit unnerving because you can tear away at these things only so far and at some point you're left with nothing standing, and I do believe an independent press is crucial," he said.

But he also points out that press credibility was an issue before Trump tried to exploit it.

The way to repair it won't be easy or happen overnight, but "we have to be authentic, reliable, and believable," he said. "We need to rebuild trust with a lot of people."

To those of us who were in Washington during the Nixon administration, there is a certain feeling of seeing a rerun of those days. As Nixon's troubles grew, we learned of enemies lists, collecting names of Jews who worked in key government departments, plots to discredit reporters, and even a bizarre plan to blow up a Washington think tank.

Even so, Oreskes believes the press today is more vulnerable than it was in those days. For one thing, journalism is more fractured than it was, and social media makes it easier for politicians to go around the traditional news organizations.

Further complicating the situation is the rise of the so-called fake news.

"*Fake news* is a bad phrase because it covers so many different things," Oreskes told us. "There's the kind of fake news that people make up because they want to produce a political result—that's propaganda. Then there's the other category—the stories that people make up because they can make money by doing it. It's a commercial thing and it's scary." (The Pope endorsed Trump and other such made-up tales popped up on European websites and were quickly picked up by American sites during the 2016 campaign, and some continue to circulate, as do the thoroughly discredited reports about former President Obama's birth certificate.)

It was this great flood of information true and false that led me to begin this book with a quotation from Oreskes, in which he said, "The scarcest resource right now in journalism is attention span. We used to live in a world of journalism governed by the laws of physics. Time and space were our key constraints: space in a newspaper, time on the air. The really controlling force in the world right now is how long you can keep your audience, your followers, consuming the journalism you are creating."

To Oreskes, that is the challenge. In the previous era, journalism was ladled out to what amounted to a captive audience. In the days before cable, network news programs had no competition save the other networks; newspapers competed against each other but had no real problem attracting reader attention. Now, he says, the journalists' first challenge is figuring out how to let people know they have important information.

In the old days of the penny press, news vendors sold papers by shouting out a catchy headline. Some modern web outlets have used a variation of that with so-called clickbait, catchy headlines that promise more than the stories below them deliver.

"If I put the Kardashians in every story we get more people to click on it," Oreskes says. "But we don't give them anything of value."

Oreskes has no plans to add the Kardashians to any of his flagship broadcasts, but to get the word out that NPR has information it believes people need to know, the organization is employing a variety of tools. It is putting more emphasis on podcasts, so much so it now believes it is the largest producer of podcasts in the world (see Andrew Schwartz's guide to the explosive rise of podcasts in chapter 17). It is also exploring ways to reach listeners on their mobile devices.

"We have a wonderful new app called NPR One," he said. "It allows you to hear both national and international news from NPR as well as from your local community, and you can get it on your phone. That's important because many young people don't own a radio.

"It's just not like the old days where the newspaper was on the newsstand or the doorstep and the news broadcast was on at 6:30 and you knew where to go to get news, it's the opposite now. We have to go out and find audiences and bring them to us. And you use Twitter and you use Facebook and you use other kinds of marketing. So there is a whole element here that has become much more intense."

Like so many of his fellow editors in the mainstream media, Oreskes has wrestled with how to identify incorrect or unsubstantiated information when it comes from high-ranking government officials who use phrases like *alternative facts*. The *New York Times* has on rare occasions actually used the word *lie* to describe such statements, but the *Wall Street Journal's* editor Gerard Baker has not been willing to go that far.

In the early days of the administration, Oreskes told us he was reserving judgment but might eventually change his mind.

"It is an important discussion," he said, "but it's less important than the fundamental issue, which is do we have the reporting strength and skill to find out what the truth is.

"That's our first job, get the facts. That's our first task."

To do that, Oreskes has created a series of what he calls B-teams that are specializing in themes that are expected to be in the news. He says a reporter has to be an instant expert on fifty different topics, which no one is, of course.

"What we want to do is to be able to turn coverage of a particular issue to someone who knows the foundational facts of a situation so that our White House people will be freer to cover Trump the man and the contacts with Congress.

"But the sustentative work on issues, we want to get that into the hands of experts as quickly as we can."

That's why Oreskes says the key remains the reputation of the news organization and its reporters. In earlier days, Oreskes says that when he used to hear CBS News or one of the other networks and reporters whose work he knew as honest and credible, that meant a lot. He trusted what they had to say.

But there are so many sources of news these days, so many news organizations, and so many other things competing for attention, it is much harder to establish a recognizable brand.

"It's much harder but that doesn't mean we should give up," he says. "We have to keep trying."

Chapter 17

———————————◯———————————

Podcast News
The Rebirth of Cool

DURING THIS STUDY I did what a friend of mine calls "a Columbus." I discovered what someone else had already discovered—the podcast. In truth so many people have discovered podcasts they have become one of the most popular features on the web. First there were books on tape, then lectures on discs and now podcasts. No news organization worth its salt is without a podcast. My colleague, Andrew Schwartz, is a devotee of the podcast and an authority on how they came to be and what they offer.

Here is his report.

By H. Andrew Schwartz

Contrary to popular belief, podcasts weren't invented by Apple; they evolved out of audio blogging at the turn of the twenty-first century. The concept was simple: listeners were able to access episodes of digital audio files that were automatically set to download to the user's computer, or to a portable media player such as an Apple iPod. That's where the term *podcast* came from—by combining *pod* for iPod with the word *broadcast*.

But back then listening to a podcast wasn't so easy. It involved frustrating plug-in devices that users needed to attach to the iPod or personal computer in order to make the podcast work.

Even if the listener could figure out how to manage the technology, the content of most early podcasts often sounded amateurish and didn't inspire many listeners. Yet the concept of the podcast remained intriguing—especially to the guy who invented the iPod. Enter Steve Jobs, who envisioned podcasting's vast potential and understood its intrinsic value. While podcasting was still in its early innings, Jobs stepped up to the plate in May 2005 with the intent of knocking podcasts out of the park.

At the "All Things D" conference, an annual gathering of techies in Silicon Valley, Jobs unveiled Apple's first integrated podcast feature: a free platform of easy-to-download podcasts featured alongside of the music being sold digitally on iTunes. It marked a seminal moment for Apple and for podcasting, as Jobs showed the world that subscribing to a podcast could be as easy as downloading a song.

The iTunes podcast platform would prove to be the next big thing, Jobs happily told "All Things D" conference hosts Kara Swisher and Walt Mossberg, both at the time columnists for the *Wall Street Journal*, the conference sponsor. And most importantly, Jobs said, podcasts would be available on Apple's new user-friendly platform from top news organizations such as NPR, who could produce premium content.

Jobs told the conference that podcasting was now ready for the big leagues.

"It's not just the *Wayne's World* of radio," Jobs said, invoking an early 1990s comedy known for its sophomoric humor. "Real radio is jumping on to this."

On our "About the News" podcast in late 2016, Walt Mossberg recalled how Jobs conceived of and executed his podcast rollout strategy.

"Steve Jobs introduced the idea of podcasts on iTunes on stage at our conference, instead of in his usual way of introducing things at his own events," Mossberg told us. "And the funny thing was he needed an example. So about a week or two before the conference, he called me and he said, 'This is what I'm going to do, if it's OK with you.' I said, great. He said, 'But I need some content. I would like you to just read one of your columns into a microphone, and we'll use that to explain to the audience what a podcast is.'

"And Steve Jobs being Steve Jobs," Mossberg continued, "being a perfectionist, he sent essentially the guts of an entire radio station down to this hotel where we were doing the conference. And I sat in this room with five technicians—it was crazy—and I read my column. And he played it through iTunes on stage."

On stage at the 2005 conference (watch for yourself by visiting everystevejobsvideo.com), Mossberg sheepishly minimized his role in Jobs's historic demo, rolling his eyes and sarcastically remarking that listening to the recording of his column was "exciting stuff."

Of course, Jobs didn't buy even a bit of Mossberg's sarcasm.

"I bet you'll be podcasting your column in the not-too-distant future," Jobs said confidently.

Last spring, Walt Mossberg retired as executive editor and columnist of The Verge (see chapter 7 for more about Walt) and hosted "Ctrl-Walt-Delete," one of iTunes's consistently most popular technology podcasts.

Despite Jobs's podcast platform launch over a decade ago, "podcasting is really a very new medium," NPR's editorial director Michael Oreskes told us on our podcast in early 2017. "It's like television in the late '40s and early '50s."

Oreskes would know. NPR has invested substantial resources to develop a first-rate suite of informative and innovative podcasts over the past decade. As Jobs had predicted, NPR recognized early on that twenty-first-century news junkies would want to listen to popular programs at their convenience as opposed to being corralled into appointment listening.

By the end of 2016, NPR wasn't the only news organization that understood that on-demand listening had become an important method of reaching consumers of news.

Major news organizations that previously had no experience with radio, or any type of audio for that matter, suddenly realized there was a growing market for on-demand listening.

And just as NPR had transformed from a radio station into a media company that also featured written online news articles and videos, traditional newspapers and television networks morphed into media companies that offered on-demand podcasts and other multimedia products.

By the end of 2016, the New York Times, The New Yorker, Washington Post, Wall Street Journal, Financial Times, CBS, CNN, Fox News, NBC, Slate, Economist, Politico, FiveThirtyEight, Vox, Mic,

BuzzFeed, and scores of other news media companies had seriously invested in producing signature podcasts.

As Bob Schieffer and I came to understand, podcasts had become an essential offering for any news organization attempting to compete in the digital age. Surely, it felt as if we were witnessing something big as premium podcasts flooded the news media landscape.

But we wondered why 2016 was the year that news-driven podcasts appeared to have been reborn as an "it thing." We knew it had something to do with the high quality of the podcasts being produced, the convenience of modern technology, the wild election of 2016, and the insatiable public thirst for news information and analysis. Yet there was another less tangible factor involved, as music industry analyst and media and cultural critic Bob Lefsetz explained.

"It's like it was in the sixties in music, the late nineties in tech, there are podcasts that are wowing us, whenever you get together with someone they ask what you are listening to," Lefsetz wrote in April 2016 in his influential emailed newsletter "The Lefsetz Letter."

"There's an underlying excitement that not only thrills you, but makes you feel proud you're a member of the club the same way you did when you were listening to FM radio and your classmates were not."

Indeed, the podcast club had opened its doors to millions of new members.

Survey data firm Edison Research reported in 2008 that just 9 percent of Americans had listened to a podcast. By 2016 they found that one-third of all Americans said that they have listened to a podcast, and about half of all Americans over the age of twelve were familiar with the term *podcasting*. Even more tellingly, over a quarter of Americans listened to podcasts on at least a monthly basis.

It's also no coincidence that the jump in listeners corresponded with easy-to-use technology like Bluetooth and smartphones becoming more prevalent and affordable. These two factors alone made podcast listening just about as stress-free as dialing up your favorite FM radio station.

In 2016, Edison Research reported that 64 percent of podcasts were being listened to on a smartphone or tablet, making it possible to listen to podcasts just about anywhere. The car, subway, and gym have become prime venues for podcast listening. Accordingly, most podcast episodes are produced in thirty-minute-to-one-hour segments—expertly made to measure for your daily commute or workout.

Not surprisingly, given the iTunes ecosystem Steve Jobs created, iPhones are the leading distributors for podcast consumption. A 2015 report by the social audio company Clammr noted that 82 percent of smartphone podcast listening takes place on an iPhone. Yet these days, Apple isn't the only platform associated with the term *podcast* any more than copying a document was once generically referred to as a "Xerox" no matter the name brand of the copier being used. Android smartphone users, for example, can access podcasts through apps such as SoundCloud, Stitcher, or Google Play.

For its part, Apple keeps listener statistics fairly close to the vest. The last time Cupertino shared data was in 2013. At that time they announced the milestone that iTunes had eclipsed one billion podcast subscriptions, that there were 250,000 unique podcasts in more than one hundred languages, and that more than eight million podcast episodes had been published on iTunes.

We asked Apple to share the latest numbers. And while they aren't yet ready to report them, estimates indicate that there are now over 400,000 active podcasts on Apple's platforms, with more than thirteen million episodes published. According to estimates, in 2016 a record ten billion podcast episodes were downloaded and streamed. In 2015, that number was eight billion, and in 2014, it was seven billion.

Of course, at this scale, there is serious money to be made in advertising dollars. Currently, the global audio market is an estimated $65 billion. And podcasting is driving that market toward on-demand audio, according to Clammr's 2015 "Future of Podcasting" study.

News organizations like NPR fully understand that podcasts have captured the American zeitgeist and possibly its pocketbook.

"We're not your grandma's NPR anymore," NPR's Oreskes told us. "Some of NPR's podcasts reach people much younger than the people listening on the radio. Some are a little more like the radio audiences. But [we're] creating these other ways of reaching people, in the way that they want to get their information.

"There's a whole new generation that's consuming their news in this new form. It's a way to reach people and it's a way to deliver longer-form journalism.

"And we don't even know yet what the potential things to invent around it are," Orsekes continued. "We have podcasts that are an individual deeply reporting something. NPR's Kelly McEvers, who does her podcast 'Embedded,' is intense, investigative-style reporting. And then we have podcasts where three or four of us sit around, and hopefully we're smart enough to say interesting things and deliver interesting information. But they're really completely different kinds of journalism, all produced under the name podcast."

NPR also places a premium on understanding who their podcast audience is and how to reach them.

"Sometimes it's about how you message that the podcast exists," Oreskes said. "You know, one of the big things that's changed in media is that we really have to reach out to the audience and say: 'Hey, we're here.' It's not like the old days, where the paper was on the newsstand or the broadcast was on at 6:30 and you knew where to go. It's the opposite now. We have to go out and find audiences and bring them to us."

As podcasting continues to evolve, our bet is that NPR will be one of its key drivers.

"Streaming audio I think will become a more and more important conversation," Oreskes said. "I think that the thing we call a podcast and the thing we call streaming audio are actually going to become more and more like each other. And ultimately there'll be a thing you can go to that will basically just give you a menu of things to get. And some of them will be more like what you used to get on the radio. And some of them will be more like what we now call podcasts. But it'll all be in one place on your phone. And we're all going to get more and more used to that."

If you'd like to watch Steve Jobs unveil podcasting on iTunes, we invite you to visit everystevejobsvideo.com and type in "Steve Jobs previews podcasting."

Podcast News

In 2016, podcasts became an addictive and useful platform for delivering the news in an unrelenting news cycle. Next we have provided a select list of podcast series about the news, politics, and technology. This list does not include podcasts that are audio replays of television or radio shows—each podcast has been produced for the audio podcast medium.

After the Fact—A podcast from The Pew Chartiable Trusts that explores the facts, numbers, and trends shaping our world.

Ask Me Another—Launched in 2012, Ask Me Another is a show from NPR and WNYC that is broadcast live on the radio and is also available as a podcast. On the show, host Ophira Eisenberg invites guests, audience members, and call-in listeners to play trivia, complete brainteasers, tell jokes, and listen to music.

The Axe Files with David Axelrod—Founder and director of the University of Chicago Institute of Politics, David Axelrod hosts The Axe Files, a structured interview with key political players. This show is produced in part by CNN.

The Ben Shapiro Show—Conservative commentator and editor-in-chief of The Daily Wire, Ben Shapiro hosts a fast-talking, off-the-cuff daily review of political headlines. On the show, Shapiro plays clips from news broadcasts, and then offers his own take on the stories of the day.

Beyond the Bubble—On this podcast from McClatchy, Kristin Roberts of the Washington Bureau hears from senior correspondents living and working in political battleground states across

America. The show premiered in January 2017 with an aim to help those in Washington understand how voters are reacting to actions on the Hill and in the White House.

Can He Do That?—Hosted by Allison Michaels of the *Washington Post* and cohosted each week by a different *Post* reporter, this show explores the powers and limitations of the executive branch. Launched in January 2017, Can He Do That? features original reporting on how Donald Trump is reshaping the role of president.

Civics 101—The creators of Civics 101 set out to help more people understand the mechanics of American government. In concise, straightforward weekly lessons released throughout Trump's first one hundred days in office, the show explains the basic features of democracy and how they play out in the United States.

Code Switch—From NPR, Code Switch began as a blog and grew into a multimedia program including a podcast. Hosted by a team of journalists of color, Code Switch is about race, identity, and its impact on the news and culture of the day.

Common Sense with Dan Carlin—New media personality and self-proclaimed "political Martian" Dan Carlin takes an independent look at politics and current events on his show. Carlin is known for his unique, staccato broadcast style.

Ctrl-Walt-Delete—Executive editor of The Verge and Recode founder Walt Mossberg hosts the show with The Verge's editor-in-chief Nilay Patel. On the show, the two talk about the modern tech landscape with a historical lens.

The Daily—Five days a week, ready by 6 a.m., the *New York Times*'s Michael Barbaro hosts a show that is responsive to the news, without reciting headlines. Launched in 2017, The Daily is a way for the *Times* to move away from "voice of God" reporting, said Michael Barbaro. "I think people are craving intimacy, and the honesty of a format in which journalists talk not just at them about the story, but are grappling with it in real time and are talking about the process they went through."[1]

Decode DC—The Scripps News Service's podcast about Washington's people, culture, and politics.

***Economist*: The Week Ahead**—Editors and correspondents of the *Economist* discuss the events shaping the world next week.

Embedded—Hosted by NPR's Kelly McEvers, Embedded takes a story from the news and goes inside it.

Face the Nation Diary—Face the Nation Diary is the latest political news and analysis from CBS News' John Dickerson.

FiveThirtyEight Politics—FiveThirtyEight founder and statistician Nate Silver talks with fellow FiveThirtyEight reporters about the most recent news in politics. The show emphasizes data-driven journalism and tracks key issues with miniseries within the show.

Fresh Air—This NPR radio broadcast, which airs on more than 624 NPR stations across the country, is also one of the most downloaded podcasts in America. It is a talk show hosted by WHYY's Terry Gross that features input from well-known critics and commentators. It's been a podcast since 2007.

Global News Podcast—From BBC News, this twice daily in the week, once at weekends show offers a selection of highlights and summaries from across the BCC World Service News.

Hidden Brain—NPR's Shankar Vedantam uses science and storytelling to explain the unconscious patterns in the human brain that prompt behavior, biases, and relationships.

How I Built This—On How I Built This, NPR's Guy Raz sits down with the founders of some of the world's best-known companies and brands to find out the stories behind their successes.

Inside the *Times*—*New York Times* Insider's Susan Lehman interviews *Times* journalists about their stories and takes listeners behind the scenes of the *Times*'s newsroom.

Intercepted with Jeremy Scahill—On this podcast from The Intercept, investigative journalist Jeremy Scahill discusses news related to government accountability and transparency. The show was founded in 2017 in response to "Trump and his cronies consolidating power."[2]

Invisibilia—This NPR show launched in 2015 is known for breaking previous records by reaching ten million plays less than one month after its release. Cohosted by Lulu Miller, Hanna Rosin, and Alix Spiegel, the show uses narratives and scientific research to explore human behavior.

Kickass News—Kickass News is a twice-weekly podcast that covers big stories in politics, entertainment, tech, business, and science through focused conversations. On the show, Hollywood producer and Republican media strategist Ben Mathis sits down with prominent thought leaders across fields.

The *New Yorker*: Politics and More—The *New Yorker*'s executive editor Dorothy Wickenden hosts a weekly discussion on politics with the magazine's writers and editors.

1947: The *Meet the Press*—Named after the year of NBC's *Meet the Press* TV debut, 1947 is a weekly Q&A hosted by Chuck Todd. Each episode features one guest, and topics touch on a number of relevant issues, including (but not limited to) politics.

NPR Politics Podcast—Launched one year out from Election Day 2016, the NPR Politics Podcast is where NPR's political reporters offer accessible weekly roundups and quick takes on news of the day.

NPR's Up First—NPR's news you need to start your day. Morning podcast focused on the biggest stories of the day. Hosted by Rachael Martin, David Greene, and Steve Inskeep.

On the Media—This weekly podcast from WNYC explores how the news is made, the marketplace of ideas, and threats to freedom of information and expression around the world.

Planet Money—Produced by NPR in association with This American Life, Planet Money uses stories to explain the economy in a way that is accessible and entertaining. The show launched in 2008, the year of a global financial crisis.

Pod Save America—On Pod Save America, four former aides to President Obama are joined by journalists, politicians, comedians, and activists for an unrestricted conversation about politics, the media, and the Trump administration. Pod Save America is a successor to "Keepin' It 1600," a podcast that churned out campaign analysis during the 2016 presidential campaign.

Pod Save the World—The international counterpart to Pod Save America, Pod Save the World is hosted by one of the same former Obama aides, Tommy Vietor. The show gives listeners an inside look at foreign policy decision making through conversations with the most influential people in international affairs.

Politico's Off Message—Politico's podcast on Washington politics.

Politico Playbook in 90 Seconds—Politico's briefing on what's driving the day in Washington.

Pop Culture Happy Hour—On this weekly roundtable, host Linda Holmes and guests talk about the books, movies, music, television, comics, and popular culture of the moment. A version of this podcast has been available on NPR since 2010.

Presidential—Starting with George Washington in week one, this forty-four-episode series from the *Washington Post* explores how each former American president reached office, made decisions, handled crises, and redefined the role of commander-in-chief. The podcast concluded on Election Day 2016, with its final episode discussing opportunities for the president-elect.

ProPublica Podcast—A weekly program featuring interviews with ProPublica reporters and information about the latest investigations published by ProPublica.

Recode Decode—On this show, executive editor of Recode Kara Swisher interviews business leaders and big-name personalities about news in the ever-evolving tech industry.

Recode Media with Peter Kafka—Recode tech journalist Peter Kafka talks with leaders in media and technology to explore opportunities for the two to collide in the future.

Serial—Serial, the first mega-hit of podcasting, propelled the medium into mainstream popularity. Following its launch in 2014, the show shattered all previous podcasting records in terms of downloads and streams. Hosted by Sarah Koenig, Serial investigates one story, in real time, over the course of an entire season.

Slate's Trumpcast—During the 2016 presidential election, many listeners began to rely on this quasi-daily podcast from Slate in order to make sense of the unusual Trump campaign. Since Election Day, Slate writers and executives have continued talking with historians, psychiatrists, and other experts to explain who Trump is, and what is happening in American politics today.

So That Happened—Each week the Huffington Post's Politics team offers its own version of the Sunday shows.

StoryCorps—Produced by NPR, the organization StoryCorps travels the country to create this podcast, where real people interview one another. These unscripted conversations are transformed into StoryCorps episodes.

The Takeout—Politics, policy, and a side of pop culture from CBS's Major Garrett.

TED Radio Hour—TED Radio Hour is a show composed of TED Talks, interviews, and commentary woven together by a single

theme per episode. Hosted by NPR's Guy Raz, the show is copro-
duced by NPR and TED.

This American Life—From WBEZ Chicago, This American Life
is both a podcast and a weekly public radio show that broadcasts on
over five hundred stations. It is one of the most popular podcasts in
the country in terms of streams and downloads. Hosted by public
radio personality Ira Glass, each episode follows a certain theme
featuring real stories from real people.

Too Embarrassed to Ask—A spinoff of the Recode Decode
podcast, Too Embarrassed to Ask aims to make technology easier
to use and understand. Hosts Kara Swisher of Recode and Lauren
Goode of The Verge explain the latest products in tech.

The Vergecast—Since 2011, the Vergecast, The Verge's flagship
podcast, has taken a weekly look at tech news. The Verge's Nilay
Patel and Dieter Bohn host the show and are joined by notable
personalities in tech.

VOX The Weeds—Vox's Ezra Klein, Sarah Kliff, and Matthew
Yglesias talk with guests about the politics of policy, getting deep
into topics like health care, economics, and zoning—or what they
call "the weeds."

Wait Wait . . . Don't Tell Me!—Another radio broadcast/NPR
podcast, on this show host Peter Sagal challenges listeners and
celebrity guests to figure out what's real news and what's made-up
news through a series of games and quizzes. (To be clear, this show
began in 1998 and became a podcast in 2006, long before fake
news and alternative facts were everyday vernacular.)

What's Tech?—From The Verge, What's Tech? examines the
overlap of technology and culture, and breaks down how and why
technology has transcended our lives.

WSJ Heard on the Street—Heard on the Street provides
global investing insight not yet evident in the news or financial
markets.

WSJ Media Mix—Media Mix is where WSJ reporters analyze the business of media and marketing.

WSJ MoneyBeat—On MoneyBeat, WSJ's Paul Vigna and Stephen Grocer "take the stuffiness out of Wall Street" with casual conversations about global market news.

WSJ Opinion: Foreign Edition—On this weekly podcast, hosts Bret Stephens and Mary Kissel comment on international affairs and the biggest news stories from around the world.

WSJ Opinion: Potomac Watch—On WSJ's politics-focused podcast, Paul Gigot and Kim Strassel of the *Journal* editorial page discuss news out of Washington, D.C.

NOTES

1. http://www.niemanlab.org/2017/02/with-its-new-daily-podcast-the
-new-york-times-attempts-to-break-away-from-reporting-from-on-high/
2. https://theintercept.com/podcasts/

Chapter 18

———————O———————

Newsletters
So Old They're New

FOR OFFICIAL WASHINGTON, one of the most popular features of the new communications landscape is the newsletter—those daily rundowns of what's ahead, what to expect, whose speaking where, what legislation is expected to be voted on, and a thousand other things that somebody needs to know. Some are aimed at a general audience; most are geared to specialists. In recent years, those who publish newsletters now make up the majority of the journalists in Washington. In his role as the chief communications officer at CSIS, Andrew Schwartz depends on dozens of them, so it was only natural that he write our chapter on this "old/new" part of the news.

By H. Andrew Schwartz

Emailed newsletters are "an old-school artifact of the web that was supposed to die along with dial-up connections," the late *New York Times* "Media Equation" columnist David Carr wrote in June 2014.

But as the discerning Carr pointed out, electronic newsletters were "not only still around, but very much on the march."

"An email newsletter generally shows up in your inbox because you asked for it and it includes links to content you have deemed relevant," Carr explained. "In other words, it's important content you want in list form, which seems like a suddenly modern approach."

With those observations, Carr had put his finger on an important trend in the delivery of news: newsletters were so old that they were new again. Only now, presented with the freshness and bright countenance of crisp digital templates, newsletters had reemerged as an indispensable tool for media companies to reach their audiences.

Newsletters are so old that they predate newspapers. According to the "Cybrarian Outpost," a Dow Jones blog for information professionals, one of the first known newsletters was printed in England in 1631. It featured stories about the exploits of British citizens who had ventured overseas.

In the United States, "The Boston News-Letter," which would go on to become the first continuously published newspaper in America, was originally published on April 24, 1704, as a weekly half-sheet, single-page newsletter printed on both sides, according to the Massachusetts Historical Society.

By the early 1900s newsletters had emerged as an essential niche news source for American businessmen concerned with developments in their industries. Newsletters like "The Kiplinger Letter" first published in 1923 provided "Forecasts for Executives and Investors."

Owned by the Kiplinger family of Washington, D.C., now, almost a century later, "The Kiplinger Letter" is still published by the family from a historic building not far from the White House.

Like "The Kiplinger Letter," many of today's electronic newsletters offer niche news.

But the noteworthy trend that we've observed is that newsletters are an important medium utilized by news organizations to set the day's news agenda for their intended audience.

The catalyst for the newsletter's resurgence was the creation of Politico's "Playbook," a Washington morning tip sheet first published on June 25, 2007. "Playbook" was something of an instant hit, and now it's a must-read, especially by Washingtonians.

"Playbook" was the invention of Washington reporter Mike Allen, who captured the perfect balance of news tips, aggregated stories, and political gossip.

Daniel Lippman, who apprenticed under Allen and is now one of the authors of "Playbook," explained on our podcast that there is a simple reason why newsletters have become so prevalent—especially in Washington where over one hundred thousand influential people now subscribe to "Playbook."

"You have to go where people want to consume the news," Lippman told us. "People are on their phones all the time. And busy people, they don't have time to spend an hour reading the newspaper, or they want to get ready for their 8:00 a.m. meeting."

"We try to help them accomplish that, and to stay aware of everything that's going on, since it's such a busy world."

Indeed, by the end of 2016, the resurgence of emailed newsletters was so evident that the Pew Research Center's annual State of the News Media study found that thirty-five out of forty digitally native news websites born on the web (like Politico) offered email newsletters.

Legacy news organizations like *Wall Street Journal, New York Times*, and *Washington Post* took note of what Politico and the digital cousins were up to. They quickly came to view newsletters as a cornerstone of their distribution strategy.

"What we found is that in Washington in particular, but not only in Washington, this is in fact how people are receiving their information," the *Wall Street Journal*'s former Washington Bureau chief and author of the *Journal*'s "Capitol Column" newsletter Gerald Seib told us on our podcast.

"They want to know what's in the *Journal* in a nutshell, and what we're trying to do in our newsletter is give them what's in the *Journal* in a nutshell," Seib continued.

"Then they have the opportunity—and we make it as easy as we can for them—to go from the *Journal* in a nutshell to the specific stories in the newsletter. It's not really unlike sitting at your breakfast table, leafing through the newspaper. You're just doing it on a screen with an email that has the summary for you, and it is a way, I think, that we just have found a new delivery vehicle for delivering our news to people. You can throw the paper on somebody's porch or you can give them an email, and they both carry the same stories and they give you the same opportunity to pick and choose which ones are important to you that morning.

"In Washington, it turns out, that is the way a lot of people consume news in the morning. They want the summary, they want it in a nutshell, and then they pick and choose, and it's become a very powerful delivery vehicle, in this town in particular."

Of course with the proliferation of newsletters comes competition. And nowhere is the competition more cutthroat than among the *Wall Street Journal*, *New York Times*, and *Washington Post*. In an attempt to move ahead, the *Times* has adopted a new newsletter product they call "Briefings," which are consistently updated and employ compelling visual journalism to entice the reader. The newsletters are designed so the subscriber can check in at any time and be informed.

The *Times*'s "Morning Briefing," for example, is published weekdays at 6:00 a.m. Eastern and updated on the Internet throughout the morning.

"Basically a briefing is a running story online that is updated as much as every five or ten minutes," *New York Times* Washington Bureau Chief Elisabeth Bumiller told us on our podcast.

"What we have found is that there are so many Washington newsletters now," Bumiller continued. "We just find that there's a lot more readership on these live briefings that you go to on the homepage or on your phone, and check in.

"And the briefings have a much larger audience—these running stories on the web. And also, because of the graphics now and the design on the web they look really good. They're very inviting. We can embed video with them, we can embed a lot of photos. They pull you in. And it's just a way for busy people in Washington—or anywhere in the world, actually—just to check in to see, OK, here's what's happening."

In addition to the "Morning Briefing," the *Times* has also created "Evening Briefing" and "Weekend Briefing." And there are distinct Americas, Asia, Europe, and Australia briefings.

Perhaps one day, we will be saying, "Briefings are so old, they are new."

Chapter 19

─────────○─────────

Stephen Colbert
The Case of the Stolen Gig

SO HERE'S A QUESTION FOR YOU: Was Stephen Colbert Donald Trump's muse?

"Well, I was on the air with the old show eight years," Colbert told me with a laugh. "OK, that's two terms. I might have been an inspiration. If so I apologize."

I reminded him that Trump does by all accounts watch a lot of television. Maybe he had gotten an idea or two.

Colbert didn't miss a beat.

"I invented the over-the-top television personality," he answered, "who desperately wants to be loved, is willing to accept emotion over fact, and has a pet eagle.

"He really is a sort of a collection of emotions in search of a purpose, and that's what my whole character was and I really do feel he's stolen my gig a little bit.

"I ran for president too. I knew it was a joke."

What Colbert does not find funny are suggestions that his comedy routines about fake news and the false stories coming from websites that try to pass it off as real are one and the same.

He has no regrets about his early work with Jon Stewart when they parodied newscasts, but "while we were called fake news, I think fake news is being transparent that you're being fake.

"What people are describing now as fake news is just plain lying. You create a completely fraudulent story without ever telling

141

people that it is a fraudulent story. There is nothing artful or beneficial about that.

"I do get upset when I hear people say this is fake news and you used to do fake news. This is beyond fake news."

We wanted to talk with Colbert for this project because late-night comics played a larger role than ever in the 2016 campaign, another reminder that Americans no longer get their news from only the traditional sources.

Going on entertainment shows to soften your image is not all that new in American politics. Richard Nixon was one of the first politicians to try it. He played piano on the Grand Ole Opry and bought down the house when he appeared on *Rowan & Martin's Laugh-In* and deadpanned into the camera, "Sock it to me?" the show's running gag. By the time of Johnny Carson and then Leno and Letterman, stops at the late shows were part of every successful presidential candidate's campaign plan.

Bill Clinton rescued his own career with a late-night stop after the horrendous evening when he introduced Democratic nominee Michael Dukakis at the 1988 Democratic convention. The speech droned on so long that the loudest and most sustained applause came when he finally said "and in conclusion."

Convention delegates left the hall thinking that if the bright and upcoming young governor from Arkansas had ever had a future in national politics, he had ruined it that night.

Within days, Clinton showed up on Carson's *Tonight Show* and with a great flourish set an egg timer on Carson's desk. He then wowed the audience with an "aw shucks" country boy performance in which he said he was just trying to get in as much as he could to help Dukakis.

Dukakis lost in a landslide, of course, and four years later Clinton was elected president.

It was Colbert's mentor Jon Stewart and later Colbert who took political comedy to a new level on the Comedy Central channel. First came Stewart's *Daily Show* on which Colbert was a cast member. As the show rose in popularity, Colbert's character—a blustering, right-wing fool—was spun off into a new show, *The Colbert Report*. The shows became so popular from the mid-1990s to 2015 that some worried they were the only place young people were getting their news. The concern was so prevalent that any time I gave a lecture, I was asked if that worried me and what could be done to correct it. My answer was nothing could or should be done. If you weren't up on the news, I said, you didn't get the jokes, so to me, the comedy shows' popularity was a sign young people were getting the news from somewhere and were more informed than they were being given credit for. I always felt that Stewart and Colbert were to television what the editorial cartoonist was to newspapers. The cartoonist is the only one on the paper who has the right to lie, which is what parody is all about—taking things one step beyond reality, which helps us understand the fallacy of false arguments and see things we might not otherwise have noticed. So it was with Stewart and Colbert. They didn't diminish our understanding of the news but increased it. Perhaps it is overstating the obvious to add that no one can be truly informed by watching only comedy shows any more than one can become informed only by reading editorial-page cartoons.

Colbert and Stewart invited politicians to be on their shows, and the invitations were seldom declined.

To borrow a sports phrase, having politicians on during an election year is good for both teams. The politician gets a chance to show voters a side they might not otherwise know, and for the shows it's an opportunity to stay on top of the news, which in Colbert's view is the number-one priority.

"The shows at their best should be what people are talking about that day," he said. "If so much of the national conversation is about politics, then the politicians become the entertainment."

The important thing, he believes, is to stay in the moment, and that's where the political guests come in handy.

"I try not to think about what's coming ahead," he said. "I try to swing only at the pitches that are coming across the plate today, and I encourage my writing staff to do the same. I don't try to write jokes for the next four years," he said. "The next four years will take care of themselves."

He admits that politicians—at least some politicians—require more preparation. John McCain is easy, he says, because he'll talk about anything. He says former president Obama was also "fairly loose."

The former First Lady Michelle Obama was one of Colbert's most popular guests, but he says her appearances were always timed to one of her initiatives. There was always an agreement, he said—he could talk about topics of his choosing as long as he brought up the initiative she was focusing on at the moment. He would usually do more research for those kinds of interviews and would sometimes do "dry runs" with a staff member.

I wondered if there is anything off limits in such interviews, such as the time on Jimmy Fallon's show when he reached over and grabbed Donald Trump's hair and mussed it up?

"Jimmy and I are different," he said. "He's a very playful guy, and that's what you expect of him. So while I wouldn't have done it, I don't think it's an out-of-bounds thing as long as the guest is OK with it. I can't imagine that happened without approval from Mr. Trump."

The problem for Colbert is not dreaming up questions for the high and mighty but just keeping up with the news in the constantly changing 24/7 news cycle.

He is still trying to get used to the speed at which stories change these days, saying, "It's like the super-positioning of a quantum particle, you don't know where the news is at any given moment."

"We have to have somebody in our writers' room looking at the news every minute before the show goes on to make sure the big story hasn't completely changed moments before we record my show.

"Because I'm not really news, I've never had to work at this pace. I can imagine what the pace is for news people because we've gone from go-kart to NASCAR in how fast the story is changing."

Colbert is not all that optimistic about healing the partisan divide.

"I don't know what's going to make it better because we're increasingly having trouble agreeing on what is real, and unless you have agreed on the reality which is the playing field of communication or debate, then how can you ever come to an agreement?" he said.

"I suppose something tragic could make us come together or some great success—going to Mars, discovering there is life on another planet, or something tragic like a war or a natural disaster might bring us together.

"But it's as if there is a fever, and I'm not sure what it will take to make it break."

Like Scarlett in *Gone with the Wind*, Stephen Colbert will think about that tomorrow. As he told us, to make his show work he has to live in the moment, and right now he's got his hands full just figuring out today.

For sure, Colbert figured out something. When the September–May television season ended in 2017, Colbert wound up atop the late-night ratings.

Except for one brief period in 2010, according to the *New York Times*, it was the first time CBS had beaten NBC in the late time slot in 22 years.

Chapter 20

─────────────────○─────────────────

Flying Solo Sooner
Training Reporters for the New Era

JOURNALISM HAS ALWAYS BEEN an apprentice-learned craft. The way to write has traditionally been best learned by attaching yourself to a better writer and doing what they say.

Generations of reporters have learned to write from editors who read every word they wrote and made corrections. But today's reporters may not always have that opportunity. Smaller staff means fewer editors. In my salad days at the *Fort Worth Star-Telegram*, at least three people read my story—the city editor, the news editor who decided where to place the story in the newspaper, and a copyeditor who corrected grammar, spelling, facts, and then wrote a headline for the story—before it went to the "back shop" to be set in type. If it was the least bit controversial, it was also read by phone to the company lawyer. At CBS News in Washington, no story goes on the air until it is read by the Washington producer, a senior producer in New York, as well as the executive producer and anchor.

Today, reporters at some newspapers file their stories to the newspaper website before they have been read by anyone. Editing comes later.

Fewer editors not only increase the possibility of mistakes but also require individual reporters to be well grounded in libel law and ethics. Learning on the job and having the backup of experienced editors are luxuries unavailable to many young journalists, and this puts new emphasis on what they need to know as they embark on that first job. It is somewhat akin to pickup sandlot sports. Sure, you can learn the game without a coach, but a coach can help the learning process.

Kristie Bunton is the dean of the Bob Schieffer College of Communication at Texas Christian University, and I asked her to tell us how all this has changed her job of preparing the new generation of journalists.

Here is her report.

By Kristie Bunton

If the 2016 presidental candidates' and voters' quickly evolving use of social media prove anything for the teachers who train tomorrow's journalists and the scholars who scrutinize the performance of today's journalists, it's these two things:

One, journalism matters more than ever.

Two, the fundamental ethical principles of journalism—telling verifiable truth, maintaining independence from sources and subjects, disclosing conflicts of interest, and serving the needs of citizens—are more important than ever.

Therefore, it's incumbent upon those of us who are teachers and study journalism to advocate forcefully for those two ideas.

Sometimes, of course, it's easier to do that than others.

For at least the last decade, whenever I speak with the parents of prospective college students, the most frequent question they ask about their students' interest in studying journalism is "But isn't journalism dying?"

I don't blame these parents for asking that question. After all, parents are faced with the burden of paying college tuition bills, or with helping their students find ways to pay those bills. Naturally, then, parents want to ensure their students gain an education that will help them succeed in the twenty-first century. Parents have heard many voices encouraging their students to study science, engineering, and business so they can be prepared for careers in such fields as data analysis or health care. In addition to hearing this advice, these parents draw on their own experience. They don't subscribe to a printed newspaper that lands with a thud on the front porch every morning, and they aren't at home watching an early evening TV news broadcast with their families. Nor are their students, the very young people who profess an interest in studying journalism. So isn't journalism dying, the parents ask?

My answer to the parents has always been simple. "No," I say, with conviction, "journalism is not dying." Then I explain my view that some of the formats in which journalism has traditionally been delivered—think of the printed newspaper—may be languishing or changing, but I believe citizens will always need verified, independent information, and that's what journalism is. Therefore, we need to teach and study journalism.

After the 2016 presidential election season, I believe that more than ever.

For our system of representative democracy to survive in an increasingly complex world in which our government acts in many arenas, we as citizens require independent, verifiable information that serves our need to know what our government—and the candidates who seek to lead it—is doing and why. That's what journalism does.

That's what it did during the 2016 election season.

Journalism—not government, not the campaigns—reported to voters the verifiable information that one of the presidential candidates had uttered despicable views about women in semipublic conversations. Journalism reported to voters verifiable information that the same candidate lied about his contributions to his own charitable foundation and the gifts he said it had awarded. Journalism doggedly followed that same candidate around the country, documenting to voters all the ways in which he seemed to play fast and loose with the truth at his campaign stops.

A logical person might ask, "So what? Voters elected that candidate anyway." Yes, they did. That's how our system of representative democracy works, and how it always has worked. Voters get to choose. That's the beauty of our system. Our country's founders put the power—and their faith—in the people. Sometimes, we the people make better choices than other times. For instance, we the people elected as presidents Franklin Pierce and Warren G. Harding. No one suggests their likenesses belong among the presidential giants carved on Mount Rushmore, and yet the United States survived their terms.

I believe it will continue to survive. But to do so, it needs journalism.

To be clear, I'm not an original thinker in that belief. Let's credit Thomas Jefferson with the famous view that if he had to choose, he'd pick newspapers over government.

But let's also remember Jefferson said our system needed not just newspapers. He said it also required informed citizens. His exact words, written in a 1787 letter, were: "The basis of our governments being the opinion of the people, the very first object should be to keep that right; and were it left to me to decide whether we should have a government without newspapers or newspapers without a government, I should not hesitate a moment to prefer the latter. But I should mean that every man should receive those papers and be capable of reading them."

Journalism. Informed citizens. Take it from Jefferson: We need both.

Presumably, journalism alone is not responsible for creating informed, literate citizens of the sort Jefferson imagined reading and understanding information about current issues. Public schools come to mind as another institution responsible for creating those citizens. But we don't get public schools without a government willing to fund them, and government generally doesn't fund institutions the citizens don't want their tax dollars to support. So that we as citizens can tell government what we want it to do with our tax dollars, we need journalism to answer such questions as what public schools cost us, how effectively they operate, and how else government could spend our dollars.

We need both journalism and informed citizens, and it's doubtful we will have either without the other.

But while we need journalism and informed citizens, we don't necessarily need newspapers or evening TV news broadcasts. Those are delivery mechanisms, and if the history of American media tells us anything, it tells us that old mechanisms adapt when new mechanisms arise. Books survived the rise of printed magazines and newspapers. Movies and radio survived the rise of television.

Granted, the older medium's preeminence was often eclipsed by the newer medium, but in each case, the older medium adapted, continuing to deliver content to select audiences, even if in a less dominant manner.

The history of American journalism, then, is a history of change. To survive the change foisted on it by new delivery systems, journalism's delivery mechanisms must change. They always have, and I think they always will. Young journalists created by universities like mine will succeed because they're persistent, adaptable professionals of integrity who embrace the challenges new mechanisms provide. At Texas Christian University, our college of communication is lucky enough to be named for our alumnus Bob Schieffer, whose own career exemplifies those characteristics. His first journalism jobs in Fort Worth were in radio and newspaper. After a few years, he leapt into the CBS network television world, becoming a journalistic role model along the way. He covered every beat in Washington, including the Pentagon, the White House, and the State Department, and then he mastered the art of anchoring both the morning and evening news, which are obviously quite different in style and content. More recently, in his "retirement" from guiding *Face the Nation* to the status of most-popular Sunday morning political news program, he became a commentator on the network's 24/7 digital platform CBSN. For this "About the News" project, he took up podcasting. I'm glad to remind our nineteen- and twenty-year-old students that our college is named for an eighty-year-old who keeps adapting.

But here's what should not change: The fundamental ethical principles upon which honorable journalism is based, no matter how it's delivered.

Those principles—telling verifiable truth, maintaining independence from sources and subjects, disclosing conflicts of interest, and serving the needs of citizens—must remain paramount.

For the most part, I think they are. What I hear in the interviews with the many journalists Bob Schieffer and Andrew Schwartz conducted for their "About the News" project is a commitment to these fundamental ethical principles, even in the face of reporting on an unusual presidential campaign and using the rapidly evolving tools of social and digital media to do so.

For instance, BuzzFeed editor-in-chief Ben Smith expresses a commitment to telling verifiable truth when he describes his site's practice of posting multiple campaign rally recordings of candidates to let readers listen for themselves to the candidates' contradictory speeches.

Washington Post executive editor Martin Baron expresses a commitment to maintaining independence from sources and subjects when he tells Schieffer and Schwartz, "We will tell the facts as we discovered them to be, no matter who is offended, no matter who takes umbrage." He points out that's exactly what the *Post* did in pushing relentlessly to undercover the facts about Donald J. Trump's charitable foundation, rather than to simply report Trump's version of the story.

Mic cofounder Chris Altchek expresses a commitment to disclosing conflicts of interest when he says his news site aimed specifically at millennial readers practices "radical transparency" in letting those readers know the site reports on marriage equality as a given idea, rather than a debatable one. Altchek then respects readers to decide whether they'll trust journalism produced by a site with a clearly identified social position.

Many of the journalists express a commitment to serving the needs of citizens when they worry aloud about the time pressures imposed by digital media's 24/7 news cycle, or the lack of "watchdog" coverage of local government, or the disturbing growth of "fake" news.

Daily Beast national security correspondent Nancy Youssef, for instance, says she worries about publishing information too quickly on a site that tells its reporters 70 percent accuracy is acceptable because inaccurate information can be corrected just as quickly as it was posted. She says, "I often say my relationship with the reader is one of the most cherished relationships of my life. I feel such a responsibility to them." For that reason, she won't accept 70 percent accuracy and pushes herself to a higher standard before posting.

CNN media correspondent Brian Stelter and *Washington Post* media columnist Margaret Sullivan also express a commitment to serving citizens when they suggest some responsibility for journalists to help citizens become "news literate" so they can discern what are legitimate sources of journalism. Stelter goes so far, in fact, as to point out an ethical obligation for informed citizens when he encourages them to resist the urge to forward to their friends outrageous fake news reports that pop into their social media feeds. Indeed, I find plentiful evidence of commitment to ethical principle from these journalists interviewed by Schieffer and Schwartz. I hear another encouraging theme as well. It's a willingness on the part of many of these journalists to confront their own failings in a public venue. CNN contributor Soledad O'Brien, for instance, bluntly suggests some journalists should be ashamed of their performance in the 2016 campaign. She says, "I've read so many reporters talking about, like, I didn't know where any of these Trump supporters came from. You know, you should be surprised at yourself, and ashamed. You know, if there's a whole bunch of people who you didn't know existed and your job is a reporter, you know, that's pretty shameful."

New Yorker writer Jill Lepore tells Schieffer and Schwartz that media organizations of all sorts must examine their performance in the wake of the 2016 election. She includes elite news companies such as the *New York Times* that have always been engaged in doing journalism but may have failed citizens by not clearly reporting what public opinion polling meant in 2016, and she includes social media companies such as Facebook that are now only reluctantly confronting their role in providing a platform for the "fake" news that passed for journalism with many voters.

Chris Cillizza (now at CNN), who started the irreverent political blog and podcast for the *Washington Post*, describes the need he felt to correct his own work. He describes writing a piece with the heading "Boy, Was I Wrong about Donald Trump" and publishing it long after he'd written a piece explaining why Trump could never win the Republican nomination for president. Cillizza says the original piece was correctly based on everything journalists and pundits knew at the time about presidential politics, which clearly suggested Trump could not win the nomination. Cillizza's piece sixteen months later pointed out his errors. He tells Schieffer and Schwartz, "Here is why I was wrong. I owe him (Trump) an apology." In the world of political journalism, that's no small admission.

This sort of desire by journalists to confront their failings suggests a commitment to the ethical principle of accountability. It encourages me to believe that whatever the yet-to-be-invented mechanisms that deliver news to citizens in the future, independent journalism will survive as long as journalists are committed to its ethical practice. We will all be better for that.

Part Three

FINAL THOUGHTS

WHAT WE LEARNED OR SHOULD HAVE—thoughts on the new world of communication, a political system sorely in need of repair, and an example of journalism at its best.

Chapter 21

———————————◯———————————

2016

Reflections on the Year That Was

WALT MOSSBERG, THE ONE-TIME *Wall Street Journal* columnist who left the newspaper to become one of the most successful journalistic entrepreneurs of the digital age, put it this way: when you're in the middle of something, it's hard to make sense of it.

Clearly, we're in the midst of a vast technological revolution that has changed our entire culture, including how we get our news. The revolution is so complex and fast moving that no one can fully understand it.

But we come away from our yearlong investigation with certain conclusions. In most think tank studies we would place these conclusions at the front of the book in an Executive Summary, which is sort of a Cliff Notes, condensed version of a report for busy government officials, specialists, academics, and other interested parties.

We have chosen to put our conclusions last in the hope that serious readers will have come to their own conclusions by now and will find it interesting to compare them with ours, to agree or disagree, and perhaps offer thoughts of their own.

In that spirit, here is what we found:

CONCLUSION: Americans are so overwhelmed by information in the digital era they cannot process it. It seems reasonable to conclude that specialists and some elites are more informed, especially if one judges advances in math and scientific fields. But there is little to suggest we are more informed politically, which is especially difficult for those in the lower-income groups. Research indicates that situation may be getting worse with increased reliance on mobile devices—a development that could further divide an already deeply divided country.

CONCLUSION: Fake news made up out of whole cloth for political or financial profit poses a growing and dangerous threat to democracies both here and in Europe, all of which depend on informed electorates and faith in traditional institutions.

CONCLUSION: The increased reliance on mobile phones and other technology has made polling less reliable and will require not only better methodology but also a whole new way of looking at public opinion sampling.

CONCLUSION: Legacy national news organizations produced remarkable journalism during Campaign 2016, but declining advertising revenue has plunged smaller local newspapers into a death spiral from which they may not recover, a situation that could produce corruption on the local level never seen in this country.

CONCLUSION: The chickens came home to roost in Campaign 2016. Our electoral system is broken, more in need of repair than our roads and bridges.

And I'll have some thoughts after sixty years as a reporter.

As we say on TV, those are the headlines, now the details.

TOO MUCH NEWS

Graham Allison, the national security expert who heads Harvard's Belfer Center for Science and International Affairs, had the best answer when I asked him if the 24/7 digital news cycle was producing more information than we could process.

"Of course it is," he said. "Think of it this way: put five people in a room and give them ten pieces of information. Maybe one or two could remember most of the information, the others could probably remember half, or maybe some would remember even less.

"Then give them twenty pieces of information; it's unlikely any of them could remember more than five or so. Then give them twenty thousand pieces, or two hundred thousand. Who is going to remember even a small part of that? It's just not humanly possible."

The always-quotable Walt Mossberg put the good news and the bad news of the news glut another way in chapter 7: "The point is, we have much more at our fingertips. But we have much worse curation.

"What was a newspaper? What was a nightly news broadcast? What was a local newscast? They were curated bunches of news stories. Encyclopedia Britannica was a curated attempt to capture most of the basic knowledge you would need about the world.

"Today we have way more journalists, way more information providers and way less curation."

The rise of fake news adds further confusion. We found little evidence that this will sort itself out in the near future and may well grow worse with increased reliance on mobile devices, especially among Americans in lower-income groups.

By 2020, 80 percent of Americans will own a mobile device, and news organizations will target them to gain new subscribers.

Research by Dr. Johanna Dunaway of Texas A&M and other scholars conclude that the "news interested" will spend a significant amount of time using news apps. But most mobile users' encounters with news are incidental and generally occur when they are using their phones for other reasons.

Exclusive reliance on mobile devices has risen sharply among minority and lower-income groups, and while mobile access to news is better than none at all, Dr. Dunaway reports, news is more costly to access by phone, and many people simply can't afford it. The thrust of a paper Dunaway prepared during a 2016 fellowship at Harvard's Shorenstein Center for Media, Politics and Public Policy concluded the following: News is a relatively small part of the content accessed through mobile devices. The "politically interested" are consuming more news than before and know more about politics than before. But news apps are often luxuries lower-income groups can't afford. For those on a small budget, choices have to be made, and news is almost certain to take a back seat to more pressing or compelling uses.

The danger Dunaway's research exposes requires serious attention: when one group of Americans is becoming more politically informed as other large segments of the population are not, it can only widen the divide in an already deeply divided country.

Dunaway notes that technological breakthroughs seldom happen without disruption, and the shift to mobile will be no exception.

Such a situation is not without historical precedent.

Writing in the *Washington Post*, Anne Applebaum reminded us that the printing press that Martin Luther praised as "God's highest extremist act of grace" led to the Reformation, the Counter-Reformation, and a century of bloody religious wars . . . but eventually equilibrium was reached.

We're not quite there yet.

FAKE NEWS

Fake news in modern America first emerged in the confusion of 9/11. Later it became the tool of jokesters, political spinners, and conspiracy buffs. But as we came to understand during Campaign 2016, it has evolved into a dangerous new tactic used by those on the political fringes and foreign agents bent on sowing confusion among western democracies for political and financial gain.

Russian Leader Vladimir Putin has long seen the efficacy of fake news. In a recent essay, Joseph Nye, former chair of the U.S. Intelligence Council and now a Harvard professor, reports that before his reelection in 2012, Putin told a Moscow newspaper that "soft power is a complex of tools and methods to achieve foreign policy goals without the use of force, through information and other means of influence."

Nye says nongovernmental forces "have long understood that multinational corporations are vulnerable to having their brand equity diminished through naming and shaming campaigns."

He says available evidence suggests that when the Russians began their intervention in the American presidential campaign in 2015, their objective was to sully and discredit the U.S. democratic process.

"The election of Donald Trump who had praised Putin was a bonus," he said.

In Europe, the volume of incorrect and blatantly false information became so overwhelming that Damian Collins, who headed the

British Parliament's investigation into fake news, said flatly, "The spread of this type of material could eventually undermine our democratic institutions."

In late February, the *New York Times* reported that a fact-checking team in Brussels created by the European Union had debunked 2,500 fake stories in sixteen months. Even so, the newspaper reported the number of false stories being churned out daily far outnumbers the 2,500 that have been discredited.

In Germany, the *Times* reported politicians and political organizations are facing a strong increase in phony stories, similar to the attacks on the Democratic National Committee and Clinton campaign chair John Podesta.

The *Times* reported that German Intelligence Agents concluded the attacks are being made by the group called Fancy Bear, which U.S. Intelligence agencies blamed for the U.S. hacks.

According to the *Times* report, German Intelligence agencies agree with U.S. Intelligence officials who believe Fancy Bear has connections to Russian Intelligence services.

One does not have to be an Intelligence official to understand that Vladimir Putin's wish list is clear. He wants to reestablish the Russian Empire, and his strategy is obvious: create turmoil and confusion in Russia's neighboring states that will eventually lead to the breakup of NATO and the eventual severing of ties between the United States and Europe. Part of that plan, obviously, is to break down, raise doubts, and undermine Western institutions, not the least of which is a free and unfettered press.

In the digital age when news travels so quickly, news outlets become easy but important targets. In short, it is easier and faster to make up stories than it is to correct them, and as we learned during the campaign, once a story—true or false—becomes public it is all but impossible to remove it from the national dialogue.

As Lucy Boyd pointed out in chapter 6, large numbers of Americans continue to believe that Barack Obama was born in Kenya.

"The persistence of the birther movement," she reported, "is congruent with research that finds a 'backfire effect'—when evidence is provided to prove political information wrong, it only serves to strengthen the ideological person's belief in the falsehood."

When mainstream news outlets corrected false information during the campaign, purveyors of the false reports would simply reply "no, the fake news is not coming from us but the fact checkers." When the news became unpleasant to the new president, he employed a variation of the same tactic. On February 17, 2017, he tweeted, "The fake news media (failing@NYTimes,@NBCNews, @ABC,@CBS) is not my enemy. It is the enemy of the American people."

The recognition by Facebook that it had to assume some responsibility for what is transmitted to its 1.5 billion viewers and its decision to organize an independent fact-checking organization was welcome news. But it will hardly end the torrent of fake news that continues across the world.

At the risk of stating the obvious, of all the changes brought on by the technological revolution, fake news is clearly the most dangerous and will be the hardest to eradicate.

Democracies depend on an informed electorate with access to independently gathered, accurate information that they can compare to the government's version of events. It is as vital as the right to vote.

Any effort by government or outside agents to impede or undermine the free flow of information is a serious and real threat to democracy and should never be taken lightly.

What is the best way to combat "fake news?" Harvard's professor Nye says 2017 provided valuable insight.

"The best response to a 'firehose of falsehoods' is not to try to answer each lie but to forewarn and inoculate against the process," he said. "As Macron's victory (in the French elections) has shown, the European elections of 2017 may benefit from such forewarnings."

POLLING

For all the advances in technology, sampling public opinion is harder, not easier, than it once was. The dean of the polling industry, Peter Hart, was right to say in chapter 3 that national polls got the popular vote right but all polls are not equal, and some state polls employed methodology that should have been questioned.

Pollsters, including those in the campaigns, stopped polling too soon. Later polling at the state level would have reflected voters moving to Trump in the Rust Belt regions.

Mobile phones and telemarketing have led to the serious problem of "respondent willingness." Less than 10 percent of those called are now willing to be questioned. That coupled with the fact that many voters no longer have landlines makes even the most carefully controlled poll suspect.

Even so, the most interesting thing Hart told us was that we have started thinking in statistics or dynamics and analytics, and that just doesn't work because analytics tell you one thing, but they don't tell you what's in people's hearts—that from a man who has spent his life interpreting the numbers gathered by his pollsters.

Hart believes that is why pollsters missed just how much integrity counted to voters in the election and why the Clinton campaign in his opinion never really heard the voters.

What surprised me about Hart's reduced confidence in data was how closely it mirrored what Harvard historian Jill Lepore had told me shortly after the election.

She said flatly we are putting too much faith in data as if it were some higher form of truth.

"I think there is actually something lost that we haven't really begun to notice and think about," she said. "With the closing down of those newsrooms in the small towns . . . we replaced a lot of beat reporting and man-on-the-street interviewing with polling instead of going to the bar and to the tavern and to the PTA meeting and talking to a bunch of ordinary people. It's cheaper to reproduce the results of a poll, and it provides the guise of greater accuracy."

In Lepore's opinion, a piece of what's lost is not just the accuracy of the stories themselves but the civic work of those interviews. The conversations that those reporters had with people face to face at community functions does a lot of the work of gluing together a civic community. We concluded:

1. Pollsters must continue to search for better technology and be willing to state publically that all polls are not equal. Broadcasters must emphasize margins of error in broadcasting poll results. Efforts to show changes in the horse race by citing one

or two point changes in a race are within margins of error and may mean no change at all.

2. Newspapers should put new emphasis on face-to-face voter interviews and less emphasis on data-based conclusions.
3. Pollsters should conduct more focus groups to augment polling.

THE LEGACY NEWS ORGANIZATIONS: CHALLENGE AND CHANGE

Despite intense criticism from both campaigns, the networks and cable continued to be where most people got their political news, and ratings increased, especially for the cable companies. One month into the new administration, CNN was reporting a 50 percent increase in viewers.

The news at the top of the newspaper world was great, but the news from the lower decks was dismal. The big two—the *Washington Post* and the *New York Times*—had a remarkable year. Between them they had most of the journalistic scoops of any significance.

More important in the long run perhaps, both were undergoing a massive overhaul, converting themselves from newspapers to technologically sophisticated news organizations dispensing news from a variety of innovative platforms. The changes and a year heavy with news resulted in huge increases in digital subscribers and sales revenues.

That was in stark contrast to smaller papers, which continued to lose both revenue and subscribers. We found little to suggest that can change anytime soon. It may be that some local newspapers will survive by doing what the *Post* and *Times* have done—shifting emphasis to the digital news product and introducing features to the local markets that the *Post* and *Times* have used successfully on the national scene. Or as CBS News Chief David Rhodes has suggested, a digital news channel similar to CBSN may also be effective at the local level.

Every news executive that we talked with over the past year told us that taking advantage of the new technology is crucial. But equal priority must be the quality of the product. Going digital in order to reduce payroll is not the answer if the product is no better than what was printed on paper.

Rhodes says success for any news organization depends on knowing something that readers and viewers need to know and figuring out how to deliver it to them.

Maureen Dowd told us in chapter 5, "With all this fragmentation and platform anxiety, we have to keep our eye on the narrative arc because the story is still the story whether it's by carrier pigeon or Snapchat."

Journalists have spent too much time worried about whether newspapers should continue to print their news on paper when we should have been worried about the story, not the surface on which it was printed. There seems little question that the decline of newspapers has had an impact on politics. In large rural areas it has not been a question of what kind of local news people were getting but whether they were getting any news at all.

The dearth of political news in so many areas poses an obvious danger: if some entity doesn't rise up to do what we once depended on local newspapers to do, we'll have corruption in cities and towns across America on a scale we have never known.

Texas Tribune publisher Evan Smith told us that he believes the closing of newspapers across Texas is one reason the state of twenty-four million people has one of the nation's lowest voter turnouts. Since 2010, Texas has ranked from fifty-first to forty-sixth in turnout. With fewer newspapers, fewer reporters are covering politics. He says paltry coverage leads to paltry interest in politics, and Smith sees a direct line from that to low voter turnout.

Smith says the press shares some of the blame for that. He says the responsibility of the press is to "tee up for busy people what they need to pay attention to.

"The media's job," he told us, "is to say, 'Stop! This is important.'"

Early in the Trump administration, CBS News anchor Scott Pelley put new emphasis on another media responsibility: to point out when government officials, including the new president, were giving out information that didn't jibe with the facts. In what became an almost nightly feature, Pelley would quote the president on some subject, then compare it with facts. Andrew Tyndall, who runs a service that monitors media content, told the Associated Press that he doesn't consider the technique commentary because Pelley follows his assertions with stories that prove his point. Tyndall rightly called that reporting.

As for the printed word, my bias for traditional newspapers is clear. I take second to no one in my love of starting my day leafing through a newspaper. But if the ancients were able to survive the switch from scrolls to books, and early readers of hand-lettered books were able to adjust to the product of the printing press, then I, too, will someday adjust to reading the paper on an iPad. It may take me a while, but I'll get there.

THE AWFUL STATE OF AMERICAN POLITICS

Tom Friedman, the *New York Times* columnist, told me a story once about going to an advertising conference where the discussion turned to the pluses and minuses of negative advertising, which the admen agreed was very effective.

So why then, one side argued, didn't Burger King go negative against McDonald's if they wanted to topple the industry leader? Why didn't they allege that McDonald's burgers contained rat droppings or deadly bacteria?

Because, the counterargument went, Burger King was trying to increase market share, not destroy the industry itself by convincing consumers that hamburgers could kill you.

Perhaps that is what has happened to our politics. As candidates have destroyed each other with decades of endless negative ads, have they managed to destroy the system itself? Not yet, but they have severely damaged it.

We have allowed the path to public office to become such an unpleasant and revolting exercise that too many times our best and brightest want no part of it. Add that to a system that was already overwhelmed by increasing demands to raise money—even membership on key congressional committees now rests in part on how much campaign money members can raise—and we find a different talent pool of those seeking public office. Not necessarily bad people, but different people.

It is conjecture, of course, and Hillary Clinton and Donald Trump won their nominations fairly and squarely under the rules in place, but when the two major parties nominate candidates that a majority of Americans neither like nor trust, something has gone wrong.

It did not come without warning. The chickens finally came home to roost. The conditions that produced Campaign 2016 were long in the making, and correcting them will not be easy.

The first priority should be to launch a new bipartisan effort to rein in campaign spending, which is making campaign consultants wealthy but producing ridiculous campaigns that offer no real solutions to the nation's problems and leave government in endless gridlock. Campaign laws are virtually nonexistent. By 1975, thirty-two people from the Nixon era had gone to jail or paid heavy fines for campaign finance law violations. All of the things for which they were convicted are now legal.

A bipartisan effort should be made to end gerrymandering of congressional districts, which have become incumbent protection districts. Nonpartisan primaries in which candidates of all parties run in the same contest and the top two meet in a run off should also be considered, the reason being that such a contest would force all candidates to move toward more centrist positions.

The greatest and most effective reform, however, will be to convince young people that holding elective office is an honorable and needed pursuit. What America needs more than political reform is political courage—candidates and politicians who are not afraid to risk losing the office they hold to accomplish the greater good. The Founders were not concerned about political survival; they worried about being hanged when they signed the Declaration of Independence. Yet they pledged their lives, their fortunes, and their sacred honor to the cause in which they believed so strongly.

The challenge we face pales when compared to the challenge they faced, but only the kind of courage they showed us can lift us from the rut into which our politics has fallen.

Some Lessons from a Long Life in Journalism

I was flattered when Chris Wallace called and asked my advice after he was chosen to moderate the last presidential debate, and my advice was what I have given to others: remember it's not about you, it's about them.

That was one of the most important things I learned during sixty years in journalism. Here are several more.

From the beginning, I've been asked about press bias. My answer is yes, there are some biased reporters, but the great majority of the good reporters I have known have been hardworking folks whose main interest was getting the story before another reporter got it. I would guess most of them identified more with the governed than the governors, but I found few who had agendas beyond getting the story right and beating the competition. That is sometimes difficult for those outside the profession to understand. When Andrew Lack, the veteran journalist who heads NBC News, told me that with all that's going on, "if I were twenty-five years old and at NBC I'd be saying 'I can't get luckier than this' but that's for the work. The challenges the country faces, that's a separate matter."

I understood because I am a reporter. That's what reporters do every day. We are professionals trained to separate our personal lives and feelings from the stories we cover. But I also understand why those outside the profession sometimes find that difficult to believe. Bias is often in the eye and ear of the beholder. Some suspect bias because they are biased and can't understand how others are not. Do I have personal views? Of course I do. For the record, I am a registered Independent and have voted over the years for Republicans, Democrats, and once in desperation for Walter Cronkite. When I offer analysis or commentary, it is always clearly labeled as such, and I have never endorsed a political candidate.

I emphasize that I can speak only for those of us in the mainstream of American journalism who follow the traditional journalistic guidelines—don't print or broadcast it unless you have checked it out and are convinced it is true. I do not speak for the plethora of propagandists, political spinners, and conspiracy advocates or others of varying degrees of credibility who now crowd the web arguing that objectivity is only that which agrees with their point of view.

Over the years at *Face the Nation*, I was often excoriated by both sides: conservatives accusing me of being a hopeless liberal and liberals accusing me of taking a right-wing view, and some just didn't like my looks, I suppose, but that is just part of the job. I learned from some of the criticism, and some brought a laugh.

Some viewers accused me of taking a partisan approach for simply bringing up to politicians an unpleasant allegation that had been lodged against them. They might have been surprised to know the politicians did not always agree. To the contrary, when politicians feel they have been unfairly accused they don't want an interviewer to ignore the issue, they want to be asked about it so they can set the record straight.

Years ago when my brother served in the Texas State Legislature, I would sometimes be furious when I thought he was being unfairly treated, but when he was praised, I thought he was getting fair and honest coverage. I look back on those days and realize I had been a victim of my own bias (some of the time), and while I have generally gotten good press myself, probably better than deserved, I admit that I have enjoyed good reviews more than the bad ones.

Criticism of the press can be unsettling to journalists; no one enjoys criticism, but we must remind ourselves it has always been a part of free speech, and as David Rhodes of CBS News reminded us in chapter 12, while we must learn from it, it is not always valid.

"Every campaign has 'it's all the fault of the media phase,'" he said. "It just arrived earlier than usual in 2016. First, it was that television elected Trump by giving him so much exposure, then it was we missed the story because we failed to take him seriously, and finally Trump won because he used social media to go around us. Well, pick your own adventure here, it can't be all three."

In truth, none of us can be totally objective. It is much easier to be fair, which means that any time we have a story, especially a story that challenges someone's character, we have an obligation to get his or her side of it.

Fairness is the realistic goal to which all of us in journalism must strive. When we make mistakes, which are inevitable, it is more important than ever that we correct them as quickly as possible.

Accuracy is as important as fairness. As Jake Tapper told me during our podcast, bad journalism hurts good journalism, and nothing hurts our credibility more than getting it wrong.

The politician's mission is to deliver a message. Our job is to determine if it is true and what its implications will be for the electorate.

We should not assume that everyone in public life is corrupt or there for evil reasons, and we should never leave the impression that we are the exclusive fount of all wisdom.

We are not the opposition party. We are reporters. Our role is simply to ask questions and to keep asking until we get an answer. That will not always make us popular, but it is clearly what the Founders intended.

I am proud to be a reporter.

Afterword

TOM BROKAW AND I have been close friends since our days of covering the Ford White House together, and I first heard this story from him about his friend Pete Dawkins, the All-American football star at West Point and later the army's youngest brigadier general.

Dawkins had been assigned to a team tasked with writing a new set of regulations for defining a proper military haircut.

After extensive deliberation on how to explain a military haircut, Dawkins said, "Why don't we just draw a picture?" They did and went on to lesser challenges like war-fighting strategies.

I've devoted many words in this book hoping to define the role of journalists in a democracy. But maybe Dawkins had a better idea. Rather than trying to define good journalism, just present an example. There was no finer example in 2016 than the work of David Fahrenthold of the *Washington Post*, who got the dreary assignment of investigating Donald J. Trump's often cited charitable activities, a project that may have told us more about Trump than any other single investigation. And there is a bonus, in December of last year Fahrenthold wrote an account of how he did it, including how he called three hundred separate charities.

I have always loved art and am an aspiring painter, and in early years when I was struggling to find a style, a wise teacher told me: "Just pick out an artist you like and copy him. You come to

171

understand how he solved the problems you're struggling with and your own style will grow out of that in time."

In that spirit and with thanks to *Washington Post* editor Martin Baron for allowing us to reprint it, what follows is Fahrenthold's story of how he did it. To young reporters I say only this: Just copy what he did and you'll be fine!

By David Fahrenthold

"Arnold and Tim, if you'd come up, we're going to give you a nice, beautiful check," Donald Trump said. He held up an oversize check, the kind they give to people who win golf tournaments. It was for $100,000. In the top-left corner the check said: "The Donald J. Trump Foundation."

Along the bottom, it had the slogan of Trump's presidential campaign: "Make America Great Again."

This was in February.

The beginning of it.

Trump was in Waterloo, Iowa, for a caucus-day rally at the Five Sullivan Brothers Convention Center—named for five local siblings who had been assigned to the same Navy cruiser in World War II. They all died when the ship went down at Guadalcanal.

Trump had stopped his rally to do something presidential candidates don't normally do. He was giving away money.

Arnold and Tim, whom he had called to the stage, were from a local veterans group. Although their big check had Trump's name on it, it wasn't actually Trump's money. Instead, the cash had been raised from other donors a few days earlier, at a televised fundraiser that Trump had held while he skipped a GOP debate because of a feud with Fox News.

Trump said he had raised $6 million that night, including a $1 million gift from his own pocket. Now Trump was giving it, a little at a time, to charities in the towns where he held campaign events.

"See you in the White House," one of the men said to Trump, leaving the stage with this check that married a nonprofit's name and a campaign's slogan.

"He said, 'We'll see you in the White House,'" Trump repeated to the crowd. "That's nice."

After that, Trump lost Iowa.

He won New Hampshire.

Then he stopped giving away money.

But as far as I could tell, just over $1.1 million had been given away. Far less than what Trump said he raised. And there was no sign of the $1 million Trump had promised from his own pocket.

So what happened to the rest of the money?

It sounded like an easy question that the Trump campaign could answer quickly. I thought I'd be through with the story in a day or two.

I was wrong.

That was the start of nine months of work for me, trying to dig up the truth about a part of Trump's life that he wanted to keep secret. I didn't understand—and I don't think Trump understood, either—where that one check, and that one question, would lead.

I've been a reporter for the *Washington Post* since 2000, covering everything from homicide scenes in the District to Congress to the World Championship Muskrat Skinning Contest. (People race to see who skins a dead muskrat the fastest. There's also a beauty pageant. Some women compete in both.)

By the time I got to that Trump event in Waterloo, I'd been covering the 2016 presidential election for thirteen months, since the last weeks of 2014. But I had the track record of a mummy's curse: Just about every campaign I had touched was dead.

I had, for instance, covered former New York governor George Pataki's (failed) attempt to get people to recognize him in a New Hampshire Chipotle. Pataki dropped out. I read the collected works of former Arkansas governor Mike Huckabee and made a list of everything the old Baptist preacher had ever condemned as immoral or untoward. The subjects of his condemnation ranged from college-age women going braless to dogs wearing clothes to Beyoncé. Huckabee condemned me. Then he dropped out, too.

I went to St. Louis to write about a speech given by former Texas governor Rick Perry. In the middle of the speech, Perry dropped out.

So by the time the New Hampshire primaries were over, the candidates I had covered were kaput. I needed a new beat. While I pondered what that would be, I decided to do a short story about the money Trump had raised for veterans.

I wanted to chase down two suspicions I'd brought home with me from that event in Iowa. For one thing, I thought Trump might have broken the law by improperly mixing his foundation with his presidential campaign. I started calling experts.

"I think it's pretty clear that that's over the line," Marc S. Owens, the former longtime head of the Internal Revenue Service's nonprofit division, told me when I called him.

Then Owens kept talking, and the story started deflating.

In theory, Owens said, nonprofit groups like the Trump Foundation are "absolutely prohibited" from participating or intervening in a political campaign. But, he said, if the IRS did investigate, it wouldn't likely start until the Trump Foundation filed its paperwork for 2016. Which wouldn't be until late 2017. Then an agent would open a case. There went 2018. Finally, Owens said, the IRS might take action: It might even take away the Trump Foundation's tax-exempt status.

In 2019. Or maybe not ever.

Owens doubted that the IRS—already under scrutiny from the GOP-run Congress after allegations it had given undue scrutiny to conservative groups—would ever pick a fight with Trump.

"I don't think anything's going to happen" to Trump, Owens said. "But, theoretically, it could."

My other suspicion was that Trump was still sitting on the bulk of the money he had raised for veterans—including the $1 million he had promised from himself.

I asked Trump's people to account for all this money. They didn't.

Then, finally, I got a call.

"The money is fully spent," Corey Lewandowski, then Trump's campaign manager, told me in late May. "Mr. Trump's money is fully spent."

But, Lewandowski told me, the details of Trump's $1 million in gifts were secret. He wouldn't say which groups Trump had donated to. Or when. Or in what amounts.

This was an important assertion—that Trump had delivered on a signature campaign promise—made without proof. I didn't want to just take Lewandowksi's word for it.

So I tried to prove him right.

I spent a day searching for Trump's money on Twitter, asking vets' organizations if they'd gotten any of it. I used Trump's Twitter handle, @realdonaldtrump, because I wanted Trump to see me searching.

Trump saw.

The next night, he called me to say he had just then given away the $1 million, all in one swoop, to a nonprofit run by a friend. That meant when Lewandowski said Trump's money was "fully spent," it was actually still in Trump's pocket.

On the phone, I asked Trump: Would you really have given this money away if I hadn't been asking about it?

"You know, you're a nasty guy," he said. "You're really a nasty guy."

Republican presidential candidate Donald Trump said he raised $6 million for veterans groups at a January fundraiser. The *Washington Post*'s accounting, based on interviews with charities, only found $3.1 million in donations to veterans groups. In addition, almost four months after promising $1 million of his own money to veterans' causes, Trump moved to fulfill that pledge.

A few days later, Trump held a news conference in Trump Tower, where he answered my other question. Where was the remainder of the money Trump had raised from other donors, four months earlier? Turns out, it had been sitting in the Trump Foundation, unspent. In this news conference, Trump announced that he had given the last of it away—and he lashed out at the media for asking him to account for the money.

"Instead of being like, 'Thank you very much, Mr. Trump,' or 'Trump did a good job,' everyone said: 'Who got it? Who got it? Who got it?' And you make me look very bad," Trump said. "I have never received such bad publicity for doing such a good job."

Because my stories had led to this angry moment, I was on *Morning Joe* and CNN and Lawrence O'Donnell. The *New York Times* and *Le Monde* referenced my work. My dad wrote to say how proud he was of me. I read pundits predicting that the presidential race itself would change. They said the old trope about Trump— that he was a Teflon candidate, immune to accountability—was now disproved.

When I came home from my last TV hit, the kids, ages four and five years, were asleep. The house was quiet. I was still full of caffeine and do-gooder energy and decided to tidy up.

Among the clutter on the coffee table, I found my four-year-old's Party Popper, a bright yellow gun that fired confetti. For some reason,

I held the gun up to my eye and looked down the barrel, the way Yosemite Sam always does.

It looked unloaded.

Then, for some reason, I pulled the trigger.

When I got to the ER, I had a swollen face, metal-foil confetti in my hair and a faint odor of gun smoke. Finally, the doctor could see me.

"I shot myself in the eye with a glitter gun," I said. I showed him the Party Popper, which I had brought with me, in case he wanted to send it off to the National Institute of Morons for further study.

I got home from the hospital with a scratched cornea and a tube of eye ointment. The next day, with some of my dignity permanently lost, I got started on a bigger story.

The idea for this story had come from our executive editor, Marty Baron. One night, as we both waited for an elevator, Marty offered a suggestion.

Why don't you go beyond Trump's promises to give to veterans, he said, and look at Trump's giving to charity, period?

The logic was that Trump had just tried to wiggle out of a charitable promise he'd made on national TV. What, Marty wondered, had he been doing before the campaign, when nobody was looking?

That reporting process started with a lot of paper.

Working with one of the *Post*'s ace researchers, Alice Crites, I went digging for records that would reveal Trump's charitable giving, going back to his early days as a Manhattan developer in the 1980s. We looked at old news clippings, detailing Trump's public statements. And we looked at tax filings from the Donald J. Trump Foundation, which had been dug out of storage by New York state.

Those two sources told two very different stories.

In the news clippings, you could see that Trump had repeatedly made public promises to donate to charity. In the 1980s, for instance, Trump had promised to give away $4 million from sales of his book *The Art of the Deal*. In more recent years, he said he would give away $2.5 million he made off *The Apprentice*. And donated the profits from Trump University. All told, the pledges in those news clips made it seem that Trump had given away more than $12 million.

In more recent clippings, in fact, Trump's presidential campaign staff said his actual giving had been far higher than that: "tens of millions" over his lifetime.

The state's records showed something else.

They showed that the Trump Foundation—which Trump had set up to give away his own money—had received only a total of $5.5 million from Trump since 1987.

So where was all that other money that he said he had been donating?

"We want to keep them private. We want to keep them quiet," Allen Weisselberg, the chief financial officer of Trump's business, had told me about the missing money. "He doesn't want other charities to see it. Then it becomes like a feeding frenzy."

Once again, I didn't want to take his word for it.

So I set out—using Twitter—to try to prove Trump right.

I started making a list of charities I thought were most likely to have received money from Trump's own pocket. Nonprofits that had received donations from the Trump Foundation. Charities whose galas Trump had attended. Causes he'd praised on Twitter.

In each case, I called the charity and asked if it had ever received a donation from Trump—and, if so, when. Then, I wrote the charity's name and its response on a legal pad and posted pictures of the legal pad to Twitter.

My list started to grow: 100 charities, 150, 200.

In all those calls, a pattern began to emerge. In the years between 2008 and 2015—when Trump wasn't giving money to the Trump Foundation—he didn't seem to have given much to other people's charities, either. The only gift I could find in that range was from 2009, when he was credited with giving less than $10,000 to the Police Athletic League of New York City.

250 charities.

As the circus of the 2016 campaign swirled around me—Twitter beefs, Trump's criticisms of a Gold Star family and a Mexican American federal judge—I stayed focused on this small slice of Trump's life. After a while, my four-year-old daughter started talking about the Trump Foundation at dinner, just because her parents talked about nothing else. "He should give the money to the people, so the people get the money," she said. "It's not nice."

I called 300 charities.

325.

This story started to remind me of one of the weirdest stories I've ever done: a 2014 tale about the federal government's giant paperwork cave. The cave was about forty-five minutes north of Pittsburgh. The Office of Personnel Management kept federal employees' personnel records in 28,000 file cabinets inside the caverns of an abandoned limestone mine. There were six hundred federal employees down there. Cave clerks. Their job was to assemble and collate paperwork from the caverns and use that paperwork to compute how much individual federal employees would receive in benefits when they retired. The cave clerks worked in an absurdist parody of government inefficiency, which was as slow in 2014 as it was in the 1970s.

In reporting jargon, I'd tried the front door: I asked to tour the mine. OPM said no. So then I went looking for windows. I sought out ex-employees, who had firsthand knowledge of the place but weren't beholden to OPM's desire for secrecy.

I found them. By piecing together their recollections, I got the story that the government didn't want me to find.

Now Trump himself was the abandoned limestone mine.

If he wouldn't tell me what he had given away, I'd try to find the answer anyway—by talking to charities with firsthand knowledge of what he had given.

When I reached No. 325 on my list, I yanked on a window, and it gave.

"They ended up purchasing a Michael Israel portrait of Donald Trump," said Matthew Ladika, the CEO of a Florida children's charity called HomeSafe.

I had called this charity—which I knew had received $20,000 from the Trump Foundation—to ask if it had ever received anything else, from Trump's own pocket. It had not. But Ladika told me something I didn't expect: the reason for that $20,000 gift from Trump's charity.

Trump had used it to buy a portrait of himself.

The portrait had been painted by a "speed painter," who was the entertainment at a charity gala at Trump's Mar-a-Lago Club. Melania Trump bought it for $20,000. But then, later, Trump paid for it with a check from the Trump Foundation.

That raised a new set of questions. Tax law prohibits "self-dealing," which is when charity leaders use their nonprofits' money to buy things for themselves. If Trump hung that portrait on the wall at one of his resorts, for instance, he'd be breaking the law. So where was the portrait now?

I asked Trump's people. They didn't respond.

I tried a Google Images search, feeding it a photo of the portrait, which showed Trump's painted face.

"Best guess for this image: Orange," Google said.

I got a screen full of oranges. Orange juice. Orange Julius. No portraits.

I kept looking, posting details of my search to Twitter. Soon I had attracted a virtual army, ready to join the scavenger hunt. I had begun the year with 4,700 Twitter followers. By September I had more than 60,000 and climbing fast. I began hearing from celebrities and even a few personal heroes, offering their assistance out of the blue. The barbecue columnist for *Texas Monthly*—an idol to me, as a journalist and a native Texan—was watching videos of other people's parties taken at a Trump golf resort. He thought he'd spotted the painting in the background (he hadn't). Kathy Griffin, the actress, called me with her memories about visiting the set of Trump's *The Celebrity Apprentice*. Mark Cuban, the Dallas Mavericks owner, was sending me links on Twitter, new leads on Trump promises.

That army—almost all of them strangers to me—never found the first portrait. But soon there was a new target and a new scavenger hunt.

"Google 'Havi Art Trump,'" said a strange voice on the phone one day, calling from the 561 area code. Palm Beach, Florida.

I did.

The Google search revealed a new portrait of Trump. This one was four feet tall, painted by Miami artist Havi Schanz. After a phone call, I confirmed that Trump had purchased it in 2014 at a charity auction run by the Unicorn Children's Foundation. Once again, he had the Trump Foundation pay the bill.

I needed to find that portrait. I turned to my Twitter followers, putting out a photo of the new $10,000 portrait.

That was at 10:34 a.m.

By early evening I knew where it was.

"The Havi Painting was at Doral National in Miami, you can see two separate pics that tourists have taken of it," wrote Allison Aguilar.

I've never met Aguilar. I learned later that she is a former HR manager who is now a stay-at-home mother in Atlanta, writing short stories on the side. Days before, looking for the $20,000 portrait, she had scoured the website for Trump's golf resort at Doral, in Florida, scanning more than five hundred user-generated photos of the resort's rooms, restaurants and golf course.

About halfway through, she had spotted another portrait in a photo, hanging on a wall at the resort.

Then she saw my tweet, saying that I was now looking for that portrait, too.

"Oh, now *that* I've seen," Aguilar remembered thinking.

The TripAdvisor photo she found was dated February 2016.

Was the portrait still there?

The answer was provided by another stranger.

Enrique Acevedo, an anchor at the Spanish-language network Univision, saw my tweet that night, broadcasting that Aguilar had traced the portrait to Doral. Acevedo realized that Doral was just a few blocks from the Univision studios. He booked a room for that night.

"I used points," Acevedo said. "I didn't want to . . . spend any money on Trump's property, so I used points." After his newscast ended, Acevedo checked in and started quizzing the late-night cleaning crews.

"Have you seen this picture?" he asked. "They said, 'Oh yeah, it's downstairs.'"

Bingo. Acevedo found the $10,000 portrait, paid for with charity money, hanging on the wall of the resort's sports bar.

"Hey @Fahrenthold just checked and the portrait is still hanging at the Champions Lounge. How much did you say it cost the Trump Foundation?" he wrote on Twitter that night.

All of that—from my first request for help to Acevedo's discovery—had taken less than fourteen hours. Together, we had discovered Trump doing exactly what the law said he couldn't do: using his charity's money to decorate his resort.

A Trump spokesman later offered the explanation that the resort was actually doing the foundation a favor, by storing its art free of charge. Tax experts were not impressed by this reasoning. "It's hard to make an IRS auditor laugh," one told me. "But this would do it."

On a morning in October, a month before Election Day, a window opened itself.

I got a phone call. It was a source, with a video.

The first few seconds were jumpy footage of a bus, lumbering through a bland Hollywood backlot. The soundtrack was indistinct mumbling. But then there was Trump's voice.

"I moved on her, actually. You know, she was down in Palm Beach. I moved on her. And I failed. I'll admit it," he was saying. "I did try and f—- her. She was married."

That was seventeen seconds in.

On the bus were Trump and *Access Hollywood* host Billy Bush. The video, I figured out, had been shot in 2005. The two men were visiting the set of NBC's *Days of Our Lives*, where Trump was to make a cameo appearance. In a blaze of network synergy, NBC's *Access Hollywood* was there to see Trump arrive. Trump and Bush were wearing hot microphones.

On the bus, Trump told Bush about trying and failing to seduce a woman in Palm Beach. ("I took her out furniture shopping," he said.)

Trump also described how he kissed and groped women, without asking first.

"And when you're a star, they let you do it!" Trump said. The thing that stood out to me was the genuine wonder in his voice. He seemed to be saying: I can't believe it either, but the world lets you get away with this.

This was not the first time Trump had been recorded having lewd conversations. BuzzFeed, in particular, had found tapes of Trump talking about women with shock jock Howard Stern. ("You could've gotten her, right? You could've nailed her," Stern asked him once about Princess Diana, who at the time had recently died. "I think I could have," Trump said.) But those had been excused, by some, because they were just words. Trump, it seemed, was playing an outrageous version of himself in public, for the entertainment of Stern and his audience.

But this video was different. This was Trump talking, in private, about his own conduct: how, when, and why he groped women. It was not a story about words. It was about Trump's actions, which these words revealed for the first time.

I first made myself into Paul Revere of the cubicles, raising alarms around the newsroom and setting people in motion. The *Post*'s video team started to edit, transcribe and subtitle the footage. They told me they would be ready to post a version of the video at about 3:30 p.m. That was my deadline.

I called NBC to see if they thought the video was a hoax. I reached out to a spokeswoman for Billy Bush and a publicist for Arianne Zucker, the soap-opera actress in the video who escorted Trump and Bush around the studio. And I reached out to Trump's spokeswoman, Hope Hicks. I sent her the transcript of the video. I asked:

"1.) Does Mr. Trump have any reason to believe that it is not authentic, and that he did not say these things? 2.) Does Mr. Trump recall that conversation? If so, does he believe there is anything that was *not* captured in this transcript that would make him look better? 3.) Does Mr. Trump have any regrets about this conversation?"

Nobody answered right away.

In the meantime, I had to start writing. The story was easy to compose, since much of it was simply repeating what Trump had said. The only problem was the bad words.

The *Post* is a fairly fusty place when it comes to profanity. If a reporter tries to get a bad word into a story, the word is usually forwarded to top editors, who consider it with the gravity and speed that the Vatican applies to candidates for sainthood. That unwieldy system assumed that bad words would attack one at a time, like bad guys in a kung-fu movie.

But in this story, we were dealing with a whole army of bad words at once. The system was overloaded. When Trump said, "Grab 'em by the p——," for instance, the editors weren't sure people would be able to guess right away what "p——" was. They added a letter at the end: "p—y."

Other words required a ruling from the bosses.

"Go find out about 'tits'!" I heard one editor tell another, while the story was being edited—Trump had used the word in criticizing a woman's appearance. The second editor left to find a higher-ranking editor who could make a ruling. "'Tits' is all right," he said when he returned.

At this point, 3:30 p.m. was getting closer.

We didn't get any on-the-record response from NBC, Bush, or Zucker.

Then we heard from Trump's spokeswoman.

She'd read the transcript. She said: That doesn't sound like Mr. Trump. She wanted to see the video. We sent it to them at 3:50 p.m., with a warning that we would publish the story soon—with or without their comment.

Then nothing. Our lawyers and editors were satisfied that the tape was legitimate and newsworthy. The story was edited and ready to go. Four p.m. arrived. Terri Rupar, the national digital editor, was walking to her desk to hit the button and publish it without comment from Trump.

I yelled for Terri to stop.

Trump was admitting it.

"This was locker room banter, a private conversation that took place many years ago. Bill Clinton has said far worse to me on the golf course—not even close. I apologize if anyone was offended," he said in a statement that arrived at that moment.

The story published at 4:02 p.m. It became the most-read story of all time on the *Post*'s website, easily surpassing the past champion, a tale about a woman from Burundi who was believed dead but returned to crash her own funeral. At one point, more than one hundred thousand people were simultaneously reading the story about the video. The servers that measure the *Post*'s Web traffic actually broke because there was too much traffic.

Afterward, Trump's deficit in polling averages increased, from a little over three points to more than five points. Prominent Republicans turned to denounce him. House Speaker Paul D. Ryan (R-Wis.) said he was "sickened."

Trump's running mate, Indiana Governor Mike Pence, was whisked out of a campaign event—viewing a collection of autographed cardboard hot-dog buns in Toledo—without comment.

Trump himself made a second, more thorough apology in a ninety-second Facebook video later that evening. "I said it, I was wrong, and I apologize," he said.

I had to buy another suit, for TV appearances. My daughter, now fully over the idea that her father was on TV, began complaining when I came on and she had to switch off *Peppa Pig*. I had to quit doing the cooking at home. (Nobody complained about that.)

On Twitter I watched myself become a minor celebrity—all because of a story that had, essentially, fallen into my lap.

"My wife says that David @Fahrenthold is a time traveler from the future trying to carefully fix the darkest timeline. I believe her," wrote James Church, a professor at Austin Peay State University.

And, after I appeared on Fox News Channel to talk about the story, I heard from a man in Milwaukee. He called the *Post* but couldn't say "Fahrenthold" in a way that the voice-mail system recognized.

He wound up in the voice-mail box of another reporter in Sports.

"I wanna kill him," the caller said of me. "Thank you."

The *Post* took this seriously. I met with the D.C. police and the FBI, and a security consultant the paper hired. She was a congenial woman, a former counterterrorism official. When she arrived at our house she terrified us far more than the actual death threat had.

"Your cars are parked too far away for a car bomb," she said, looking out the front windows at the street. "They'll probably cut your brake lines." She recommended having a car patrol the neighborhood. She recommended a safe room.

She recommended stocking the safe room with provisions, in case we were under siege so long that we needed snacks.

I had to get back to work. My wife—who hadn't complained about any of this, the long hours or the missed bedtimes or the early-morning TV appearances—stopped me, shaken at what I'd gotten us into.

When the leaked Trump video still seemed to have swung the 2016 campaign, I was interviewed by a German reporter, who asked, "Do you have the feeling . . . 'This is it, this is the peak of my career'?"

The point of my stories was not to defeat Trump. The point was to tell readers the facts about this man running for president. How reliable was he at keeping promises? How much moral responsibility did he feel to help those less fortunate than he?

By the end of the election, I felt I'd done my job. My last big story about Trump started with an amazing anecdote, which came from a tip from a reader. In 1996, Trump had crashed a ribbon-cutting ceremony for a charity opening a nursery school for children with AIDS. Trump, who had never donated to the charity, stole a seat onstage that had been saved for a big contributor.

He sat there through the whole ceremony, singing along with the choir of children as cameras snapped, and then left without giving a dime.

"All of this is completely consistent with who Trump is," Tony Schwartz, Trump's co-author on his 1987 book *The Art of the Deal*, told me. "He's a man who operates inside a tiny bubble that never extends beyond what he believes is his self-interest.

"If your worldview is only you—if all you're seeing is a mirror—then there's nobody to give money to," Schwartz said. "Except yourself."

Election Day came. I thought my time with Trump had come to an end.

That night, my job was to co-write the main web story about the election. My colleague Matea Gold and I were supposed to pre-write stories for all the likely outcomes. I volunteered to write the one that said "Trump wins."

Based on the polling data, it felt fantastical and pointless, like designing a Super Bowl ring for the Cleveland Browns.

"Biggest upset of the modern era?" I asked *Post* political reporter Dan Balz, trying to use the right tone in this story that nobody would ever read. Balz said that was right.

Then the polls started to close.

And it turned out that I am not a time traveler.

About 10 p.m., as the tide turned against Clinton, the editors started killing or reshaping stories they had assigned hours before. They axed CLINTON, a story about the history Clinton would make as the first woman to win the White House. They ordered a rewrite of GOP, which was supposed to tell readers how—with Trump defeated—the GOP was licking its wounds and looking ahead to 2020. Across the newsroom, paragraphs were being deleted en masse. An entire presupposed version of the future was disappearing. It wasn't the future after all.

Finally, at 2:32 a.m., the Associated Press called Wisconsin. Trump was over the top.

"PUB TRUMP WINS STORY," I wrote to the editors, giving the order to publish the story I'd written earlier.

"Donald John Trump has been projected as the winner of the presidential election, according to the Associated Press. . . . His victory on Tuesday was the biggest surprise of the modern presidential era."

That night, I arrived home about 4 a.m. to a quiet house. I found a stale beer in the back of the fridge.

In the past, I'd always been able to step out of my job at times like this.

No matter how big the day's story was, there was always a bigger world, which was still spinning unaffected by the murder I'd covered in Northeast Washington or the natural disaster or the congressional vote I'd just witnessed. But this story was too big to step out of.

As I sat on the couch with my nasty pale ale, it occurred to me that I would be living *in* the story, from that point on.

A few days later, I was interviewed by another German reporter. He asked if these past nine months, the greatest adventure in my life as a journalist, had been for naught.

"Do you feel like your work perhaps did not matter at all?" he said.

I didn't feel like that.

It *did* matter. But, in an election as long and wild as this, a lot of other stories and other people mattered, too. I did my job. The voters did theirs. Now my job goes on. I'll seek to cover Trump the president with the same vigor as I scrutinized Trump the candidate.

And now I know how to do it.

Acknowledgments

I ALWAYS THOUGHT the best part of journalism is what you learned from those you interviewed, and after all my time as a reporter, as we put this book together, I learned things I never knew about the craft I've been practicing all my adult life.

As we plunged into the interviews and podcasts that make up the core of the reporting for this book, I knew journalism was changing, I just didn't understand how much. I knew newspapers were in trouble, I just didn't comprehend how serious the problems really were. And I had little knowledge of what was happening on the web and just how mindboggling the changes were in how we get our information. For helping me understand what was happening on the web, I thank my friend Andrew Schwartz of CSIS. He knows as much about the new communications landscape as anyone I know, as the three chapters he wrote will attest. He was a wonderful teacher.

A big thanks as well to Lucy Boyd, whose chapter on fake news is one of the most important parts of this book, and to Kristie Bunton, who reminds us that it is more important than ever to ensure that young journalists have the proper training before they take their first jobs.

Andrew and I especially want to thank John Hamre, who runs the Center for Strategic & International Studies and whose idea it was to explore how people get their news and the impact that is having on not only journalism but also all aspects of American life from our culture to our national defense. He is truly one of Washington's wise men.

Nicole Sganga of CBS News provided invaluable help to me in organizing the chapters and production of the manuscripts.

Thanks also to the CSIS team of Brandon Schwartz, Colm Quinn, Fran Burkham, Rebecka Shirazi, Ian Gottesman, Caroline Amenabar, Sofie Kodner, and CSIS interns Margaret Carlson, Brad Hoiberg, and Jamie Albaum, who helped with the research and production of our podcasts.

Andrew sends special thanks as well to CSIS executive vice president Craig Cohen for his friendship, expert advice, and always sound judgment. And a big thanks to Apple's Steve Wilson for his stellar podcast guidance.

Writing this book gave me a new appreciation for those who cover the media beats, so a shout-out as well to David Bauder of the Associated Press, Margaret Sullivan and Paul Farhe at the *Washington Post*, Jim Rutenberg and Michael Grynbaum of the *New York Times*, Brian Stelter of CNN, Hal Bodeker of the *Orlando Sentinel*, David Zurawik of the *Baltimore Sun* and Howard Kurtz of Fox News. Journalism is the most publically self-correcting of all our institutions and covering the media used to be the job no reporter wanted, but it has become one of the most important parts of journalism.

Finally, thanks to my longtime partner on *Face the Nation*, executive producer Mary Hager. I couldn't be more proud of what she and John Dickerson are doing with the broadcast. She still finds time to give me good advice.

Index

ABCnews.com.co, 53, 54
Abramson, Jill, 25
accuracy, 169
Acevedo, Enrique, 180
AdSense, 55, 59–60
African Americans: protest
    coverage for, 117; The Root
    and, 115; slang and idioms for,
    116; social media for, 116;
    Twitter and, 115–16
After the Fact, 129
Agnew, Spiro, xi
Aguilar, Allison, 180
Ailes, Roger, 107
Alefantis, James, 60
Al-Jazeera America, 97
Allison, Graham, 158
AllThingsD.com, 66
"All Things D" conference, 124
Altcheck, Chris, 43, 45; on media
    for millenials, 44
alternative facts, 122
amateur professionals, 23
Amazon, 68

Applebaum, Anne, 160
Apple platforms: iPod and, 123;
    iTunes and, 124; listener
    statistics for podcasts on, 127.
    See also Jobs, Steve
The Art of the Deal (Schwartz, T.,
    and Trump, D.), 176, 185
Ask Me Another, 129
Associated Press, 59
audio blogging, 123
The Axe Files with David Axelrod,
    129
Axios, 46

backfire effect, 57
Balz, Dan, 15, 185; on Trump, D.,
    and modern era, 16
Bankoff, Jim, 39–40
Bannon, Stephen K., xi, xii, 104
Baquet, Dean, 81, 83
Baron, Martin, 9, 42, 73; on beat
    reporters, 31–32; on content and
    mobile mediums, 74; customer
    engagement funnel for, 76–77;

Baron, Martin (continued)
    independence for, 152; on print,
    72; Trump, D., charity giving
    and, 176
beat reporters: Baron on, 31–32;
    campaign, 76; *Post,* for
    presidential campaign, 76;
    Washington, 28
behavioral science, 60
Belton, Danielle, 115; "The Black
    Snob" started by, 116; opinion
    and news for, 117; on
    presidential campaign and
    stages of grief, 118
The Ben Shapiro Show, 129
Beyond the Bubble, 129–30
Bezos, Jeff, 34, 71
bias, 4; cable news and, 110;
    editorials and, 94; fake news
    and preexisting, 60, 61; press,
    167–68
birther movement, 57
Black Lives Matter, 43; coverage
    of, 117
"The Black Snob" (Belton), 116
The Blaze, 46
Boston Globe, 73
"The Boston News-Letter," 138
Boyd, Lucy, xii, 11; on fake news
    in 2016 election, 53
Breitbart News, 46–47
Brock, Bill, 6–7
Brokaw, Tom, 104, 171
Brzezinski, Mika, 15
Bumiller, Elisabeth, 79; newspaper
    and digital content for, 80–81;
    on Tweets, 80
Bunton, Kristie: on 2016 election
    and reporters, 153; on funda-
    mental ethical principles of
    journalism, 148–49, 151–53,

154; government and journalism
    for, 150; news platforms for,
    149, 150–51; Schieffer and,
    151; on Trump, D., 149
Bush, Barbara, 19
Bush, Billy, 181–83
Bush, George W., 52;
    Guantanamo criminal release
    by, 87
Bush, Jeb, 13
Business Insider, 47
Bustle, 47
BuzzFeed, 47; on fake news in
    2016 election, 54; Russia
    blackmail documents released
    by, 112; scale of, 42; viral
    content and, 41

cable news, 1; audience decline
    for, 108; audience demographics
    for, 40; bias and, 110; non-stop
    coverage on, 109; opinion-
    based, 6; presidential campaign
    and Sunday shows on, 110;
    viewer age for, 108. *See also*
    CNN; Fox News; MSNBC
Cameron, David, 15
campaign laws, 166
Can He Do That?, 130
Carr, David, 137–38
Carson's *Tonight Show,* 142
CBS Evening News: anchors of, 9;
    Cronkite at, 9, 25, 28; Edwards
    on, 9–10; Rhodes on, 99–100
CBSN, 9, 100, 101; election night
    streaming of, 98–99; Rhodes on
    success of, 99. *See also* Rhodes,
    David
CBS News, xii, 98, 101; CBSN for,
    9, 10; Current TV purchased by,
    97; Evening News of, 9–10;

Pelley at, 165; radio news and, 9; Washington beat reporters of, 28. *See also* CBS Evening News; Rhodes, David

Center for Strategic & International Studies (CSIS), xii, 5. *See also* Hamre, John; Schwartz, Andrew

Chicago Tribune, 31

church and state. *See* opinion and editorial pages

Cillizza, Chris, 74; on news and analysis, 75; Trump, D., victory story by, 153

citizen gadflies, 32

Civics 101, 130

clickbait, 121

Clinton, Bill, 5, 142

Clinton, Hillary: Democratic populism and, 89; email investigation of, 13, 18–19, 34; MSNBC and, 110; pizzagate conspiracy and, 55–56; speaking fees for, 13; trust of, 22, 23; walking rope corral for, 16

Clinton campaign (2016): Hart on, 22–23; press criticism by, xi, 100

CNN, 108, 110; audience age for, 40; Gulf War and, 28; and Russia hacking and election, 111–12; Trump, D., exposure on, 109. *See also* Tapper, Jake

Code Switch, 130

Colbert, Stephen: on *The Colbert Report*, 142–43, 144; fake news and, 141–42; on partisan divide, 144–45; as Trump, D., muse, 141

The Colbert Report, 142–43; Obama, M., on, 144

Cold War, 56

Common Sense with Dan Carlin, 130

Communism, 66

conspiracy theories and theorists, 56, 60

Conway, Kellyanne, 53–54

corruption, 34; local level, 158, 164

Cronkite, Walter, 9, 25, 105; fame of, 28

Crosby, Lynton, 15

Cruz, Ted, 13, 89

CSIS. *See* Center for Strategic & International Studies

Ctrl-Walt-Delete, 130

curation, 67

Current TV, 97

Cutter, John, 32–33

The Daily, 130–31

The Daily Beast, 47, 152

Dallas Morning News, 92

Dawkins, Pete, 171

Dead Cat Strategy, 15

Decode DC, 131

Democratic National Committee (DNC), 34–35

design, 40

Dickens, Charles, 107, 108

digital advertising, 33

digital natives: Mitchell on, 39; newsletters and, 139; news sources for, 38–39, 46; Pomeroy on, 38

digital reporting: analysis in, 75; digital advertising in, 33; mediums in, 74; smartphone and, 37; statistics on, 38; style for, 74–75; *Times* schedule for, 80; 24/7 news cycle in, 152 digital wave, 4; attention span and, 121; big newspapers and, 8–9; BuzzFeed and, 41–42; Dowd on, 38; finding audience in, 121–22; information overload and, 152, 157, 158, 159. 67; journalism and, 149–50; legacy media and, 46, 63; major broadcasters and, 9; Mic and, 43–45, 48; Oreskes on going back to basics in, 119; Schwartz, A., on, 37–38; Vox Media and, 39–40. *See also* digital natives; digital reporting

DNC. *See* Democratic National Committee

Donald J. Trump Foundation: Owens on, 174; tax filings of, 176; Trump, D., donations to, 177; Trump, D., portrait paid for by, 178; veteran groups fundraising and, 172–75

Dowd, Maureen, 164; on digital wave, 38; on presidential campaign, 16

Dunaway, Johanna, 28; on partisan divide, 159–60

Echo, 68

Economist: The Week Ahead, 131

editors, 147

Edwards, Douglas, 9–10

Ehrlichman, John, 85

electoral processes, 3, 158

embedded, 131

Encyclopedia Britannica, 67, 159

entertainment shows: fake news and, 141, 143; politicians on, 142, 143. *See also* Colbert, Stephen

EpiPen, 23

Facebook, 45; fake news and, 59, 60, 161; as news source, 60; *New York Times* newsfeed videos for, 8

Face the Nation, 168

Face the Nation Diary, 131

fact checking, 17; alternative facts and, 122; Pelley on, 165

Fahrenthold, David, 76, 96, 171; death threat for, 184; election campaign stories by, 173; election win impact on, 186; election win story by, 185–86; glitter gun incident for, 175–76; groping women video with Bush, Billy, and Trump, D., story by, 181–84; paperwork cave story by, 178; portraits of Trump, D., search by, 178–81; Trump, D., charity giving story and, 176–79; Twitter used by, 174, 177, 179, 180, 184; veteran groups fundraising by Trump, D., story by, 172–75

fairness, 169

fake news, 10, 158; bias and, 60, 61; Boyd on, 53; Colbert on, 141–42; democracy and, 162; election outcome and, 59; entertainment shows and, 141, 143; in Europe, 160; examples of, 7; Facebook and, 59, 60, 161; Google and, 59–60; Lack on, 105; left-leaning, 58–59; mobile devices and, 159; 9/11 attacks and, 51–52; Oreskes on, 120–21; pattern for, 54; pizzagate conspiracy as, 55–56; profits for, 54, 120; Rice, J., as, 52; Sandy Hook tragedy and, 56, 60; social media and, 55, 61;

Trump, D., tweeting about, 161; Twitter and, 59; as viral, 55
Fallon, Jimmy, 144
Fancy Bear, 160–61
FiveThirtyEight, 47
FiveThirtyEight Politics, 131
The Fix, 74–75
Fort Worth Star-Telegram, 27, 31, 93
Founders, of U.S. Constitution, 8, 52, 167
Fox News, 6; Ailes at, 107; audience age for, 40; O'Reilly sexual harassment suits and, 108; Trump, D., on, 14, 109; Trump, D., skipping debate for, 172; 2016 ratings for, 107
free speech, 7, 60; criticism and, xi, 168–69
Fresh Air, 131

gatekeeper era, of news, 6
gerrymandering, 94–95, 166
Global News Podcast, 131
Google: AdSense of, 55, 59–60; fake news and, 59–60
Gore, Al, 97, 98
Gorsuch, Neil, 59
Great Recession, 30
groping women video of Trump, D., and Bush, Billy, 181–84

Haberman, Maggie, 34, 81–82
Hamre, John: as deputy secretary of defense, 5; on journalism as national security issue, 5, 11
Harris, John, 10
Hart, Peter, 21; on Clinton Campaign, 22–23; technology and polling for, 24, 162; on 2016 mistakes of pollsters, 22

Hearst, William Randolph, 26
Hewitt, Hugh, 58
Hidden Brain, 131
Hofstadter, Richard, 57, 58; The Paranoid Style in American Politics by, 56
How I Built This, 131
Huffington, Arianna, 47–48
Huffington Post, 47–48
Huntley, Chet, 28

Independent Journal Review, 48
information overload, 157; Mossberg on, 67, 159; 24/7 news cycle and, 152, 158
Inside The Times, 132
Intercepted with Jeremy Scahill, 132
International Business Times, 48
investigative reporting, 4, 32
Invisibilia, 132
Iowa, 172, 173
iPod, 123
Israel, Michael, 178

Japan: Mattis on, 82–83; Trump, D., on, 81–82
Jefferson, Thomas, 150
Jobs, Steve, 124; podcasts unveiled by, 129
Journal. See Wall Street Journal

Kardashian family, 121
Kelly, Megyn, 23, 97, 107
Kennedy, Dan, 76–77
Kennedy, John F., 26–27
Kickass News, 132
"The Kiplinger Letter," 138
Kuralt, Charles, 105
Kushner, Jared, 87–88

Lack, Andrew (Andy), 111, 167;
on 2016 campaign, 103–4;
awards of, 103; on fake news,
105; on media skepticism,
104–5; partisan divide and
news sources for, 106
Ladika, Matthew, 178
Lanzone, Jim, 98
Lefsetz, Bob, 126
legacy media, 163–65; BuzzFeed
and, 42; digital wave and, 46,
63; newsletters and, 139;
presidential campaign and,
158. *See also* CNN; *New York
Times*; *Wall Street Journal*;
Washington Post
Lepore, Jill, 162–63
Lewandowski, Corey, 174
libel law and ethics, 147
license for journalism debate, 7
Lippman, Daniel, 138
Loeb Award, 66
Los Angeles Times, 31
lower-income groups, 157–58, 159
Luksic, Andronico, 87–88

machine learning, 68
Manafort, Paul, 34
Marshall, George, 56–57
Marshall Plan, 57
Mashable, 48
Mattis, James, 82–83
McCain, John, 14, 23
McCarthy, Joseph, 56
McCarthyism, 56
media criticism and credibility:
Oreskes on, 120; in presidential
campaign, xi, xii, 100, 104;
Trump, D., and, xi, 100, 113
media skepticism, 104–5

Mic, 48; apps of, 45; growth
pattern of, 44–45; philosophy
of, 43. *See also* Altcheck, Chris
millennials, 43; Altcheck on media
for, 44; news sources for, 39–44
Mitchell, Amy, 32, 39
mobile devices and smartphones,
37; content and, 74; fake news
and, 159; global access to, 8–9,
72; as hyperpersonalized TV,
44; podcasts and, 126–27, 128;
political information and, 157–
58; polling and, 24, 158, 162
Monday night massacre. *See* Yates,
Sally
Moonves, Leslie, 74
Mossberg, Walt, 124–25, 157;
curation for, 67; on information
overload, 67, 159; on machine
learning, 68; off-platform
publishing for, 67; Pearlstine
and, 65–66; on privacy, 69; Vox
Media and, 66; *Wall Street
Journal* career of, 65
MSNBC, 108; Clinton, H., and,
110; liberal reputation of, 111;
Morning Joe of, 15. *See also*
Scarborough, Joe
Murdoch, Rupert, 31, 86, 89
Murdoch family: Fox News and,
108; *Wall Street Journal* and, 85
Murrow, Ed, 9

Nakashima, Ellen, 34
National Public Radio (NPR), 54;
Oreskes on, 119; podcasts of,
121, 125, 128
national security: journalism and,
5, 11; Mossberg on, 66
Naughton, Jim, 6

NBC, 181; Evening News, 28; News, 97, 107. *See also* Lack, Andrew
negative advertising, 165–66
newsletters: competition and, 140; legacy media and, 139; Lippman on, 138–39; origins of, 138; reemergence of, 137–38
newspapers, 149; Abramson on pleasure of, 25; advertising for, 26, 68; closing and cutbacks for, 30, 31, 91, 93; Great Recession and, 30; Kennedy death changing, 26–27; in mid-nineteenth century, 25–26; partnerships for, 34; print circulation for, 10; printing press for, 30; race and, 118; in rural America, 4; smaller, 164; Texas cutbacks for, 91, 93, 165; in World War II, 26
newspapers, local: closing of, 30–31; corruption and, 158, 164; new technology and, 10
news sources: for digital natives, 38–39, 46; employee statistics at, 42; Facebook as, 60; for millennials, 39–44; partisan divide and, 106; presidential campaign and, 29, 37, 38; recognizable brand of, 122; regional, 4; social media as, 29, 54. *See also* cable news; digital reporting; newspapers; radio news
Newtown tragedy. *See* Sandy Hook school shooting tragedy
The New Yorker: Politics and More, 132

New York Times (Times), 76, 163–64; Abramson at, 25; briefings for, 140; digital schedule of, 80; DNC email hacking story by, 83; Dowd at, 16; Facebook newsfeed videos by, 8; Haberman at, 81–82; newspaper schedule of, 79; readership of, 81; Trump, D., interviews with, 34; Vietnam War and, 27–28; web traffic for, 72. *See also* Bumiller
New York Times Magazine, 7
Nielsen, 40
9/11 attacks: false information in, 51–52; Sears Tower plane and, 51–52
1947: *The Meet the Press*, 132
Nixon, Richard, xi; on entertainment shows, 142; Oreskes on, 120
Nixon era: campaign finance law violations in, 166; Saturday Night Massacre in, 85
NPR. *See* National Public Radio
NPR Politics Podcast, 132

Oakland Tribune, 30
Obama, Barack: birth place of, 57; Guantanamo criminal release by, 87
Obama, Michelle, 144
O'Brien, Soledad, 153
off-platform publishing, 67
O. J. Simpson trial, 3
online reporting. *See* digital reporting
On the Media, 132
opinion and editorial pages: Belton on, 117; bias and, 94; *Journal*

opinion and editorial pages
(*continued*)
separating news from, 85; of
Post, 86
opinion-based radio and cable
outlets, 6
O'Reilly, Bill, 108
Oreskes, Michael: alternative facts
and, 122; audience attention
span and, 121; career of, 119;
on fake news, 120–21; on
media credibility, 120; on
podcasts, 125, 128
Orlando Sentinel, 32–33
Orlando shooting (2016): Cutter
on, 32–33; online reporting of,
33
Owens, Marc S., 174

paperwork cave story, 178
*The Paranoid Style in American
Politics* (Hofstadter), 56
partisan divide, 5; Colbert on, 144–
45; Dunaway on, 159–60; news
sources and, 106; presidential
election and, 3, 17, 106
Pearlstine, Norman, 65–66
Pelley, Scott, 165
People magazine, 58–59, 60
Pew Foundation: election news
and, 29; 2016 State of the
News Media report of, 29–30.
See also Mitchell, Amy
pizzagate conspiracy: Alefantis
and, 60; as fake news, 55;
Welch reaction to, 55–56
Planet Money, 133
"Playbook," 138
podcasts, 129–36; in 2016, 125–
26; advertising for, 127–28;
audience for, 126, 127, 128;

evolution of, 123; Jobs and,
124; of NPR, 121, 125, 128;
Oreskes on, 125; smartphone
and, 126–27, 128; The Verge,
49, 125
Pod Save America, 133
Pod Save the World, 133
political courage, 167
Politico, 10, 48
Politico Playbook in 90 Seconds,
133
Politico's Off Message, 133
polling: margins of error for, 21–
22; mobile phones and, 24,
158, 162; new methodology for,
24; Rust Belt and, 22;
technology improving for, 163;
Trump, D., and, 14, 183. *See
also* Hart
Pomeroy, James, 38
Pop Culture Happy Hour, 133
populism, 58, 88
Post. See Washington Post
post-truth, 17
presidential campaign (2016), 1,
133; Bunton on reporters in,
153; Bush, J., fundraising in,
13; Cruz in, 13, 89; debates of,
107; distrust in, 4, 166; DNC
email hacking in, 34–35; Dowd
on, 16; election win stories for,
185–86; electoral system in,
158; Fahrenthold reporting on,
173; Lack on, 103–4; legacy
media and, 158; media blame
in, xi, xii, 100, 169; negative
feelings toward candidates in,
19, 22; news sources in, 29, 37,
38; partisan divide in, 3, 17,
106; pollsters in, 21–22; *Post*
beat reporters for, 76; press

blamed in, 17; rigged election, 57–58; Russia hacking and, 111–12; Scarborough and, 111; Seib on Trump, D., victory in, 89; size of body parts argument in, 18; stages of grief in, 118; Sunday shows in, 110; Trump, D., strategy in, 14. *See also* Clinton, Hillary; Clinton Campaign; fake news; Trump, Donald
print circulation, 10
printing press, 30
privacy, 69
ProPublica Podcast, 133
Protestant Reformation, 30
Pulitzer, Joseph, 26
Putin, Vladimir: Russian Empire and, 161; Trump, D., as apologist for, 14

Quartz, 48–49

radio news, 74; CBS News and, 9; opinion-based, 6
Rather, Dan, 103
Raw Story, 49
Recode, 66
Recode Decode, 134
Recode Media with Peter Kafka, 134
Republicans: Texas and, 95; Trump, D., and, 14
reverse image search, 60
Rhodes, David, 9, 164; on CBS Evening News, 99–100; of CBSN, 99; Current TV purchase and, 97; media blame for, 100; on New York, 101; streaming for, 98, 100–101; on success of CBSN, 99

Rice, Condoleezza, 52
Rice, Jerry, 52
Richards, Lucy, 56
The Root, 49; African American influencers and, 115; launch of, 117. *See also* Belton, Danielle
Root.com. *See* The Root
Rust Belt, 22

Sachs, Goldman, 13
Salon, 49
Sanders, Bernie, 13; populism and, 88; press criticism by, 100
Sandy Hook school shooting tragedy: fake news and, 56, 60; Richards threats after, 56
Sanger, David, 34, 81, 83
Saturday Night Massacre, 104
Scarborough, Joe, 15, 17; on Trump, D., as ideologically unmoored, 17; 2016 campaign for, 111
Schanz, Havi, 179
Schieffer, Bob, 151
Schwartz, Andrew, xii, 5, 11; on digital wave, 37–38; newsletters for, 137; on podcasts, 123
Schwartz, Tony, 176, 185
Sears Tower, 51–52
Seib, Gerald, 86; newsletters and, 139; on populism, 88–89; on Trump, D., victory, 89; White House coverage and, 88
self-dealing, 179, 180
Serial, 134
sexual harassment: Ailes and, 107; O'Reilly and, 108
60 Minutes, 103
Slate, 49; Trumpcast, 134
smartphones. *See* mobile devices and smartphone

Smith, Ben: at BuzzFeed, 41–42; on print, 42–43; on Russia blackmail and Trump, D., 112; verifiable truth for, 151–52

Smith, Evan, 91, 92; on Democrats in Texas, 95–96; on gerrymandering, 94–95; state capital reporting for, 93; on voter turnout, 94

Snopes.com, 59

socialism, 13

social media: African American slang and idioms and, 116; fake news and, 55, 61; media vulnerability and, 120; as news source, 29, 54; politics and, 5; Vox Media and, 39

So That Happened, 134

Spotlight, 73

Springer, Jerry, 23

Stelter, Brian, 152–53

Stern, Howard, 181–82

Stewart, Jon, 141, 142

StoryCorps, 134

streaming, 6; of CBSN, 98–99; local level and, 10; Rhodes on, 98, 100–101

Swisher, Kara, 66

The Takeout, 134

Tankersley, Jim, 4

Tapper, Jake, 109; on bad and good journalism, 169; presidential campaign and Sunday shows for, 110; Russia blackmail documents and, 112–13

Taylor, Arthur, 85

technology revolution. *See* digital wave

TED Radio Hour, 134

telemarketing, 24

television news: generational divide for, 29; Golden Age for, 28; Kennedy death and, 26–27

terrorism, 5

Texas: closing and cutbacks for newspapers in, 91, 93, 165; *Dallas Morning News* in, 92; Democrats in, 95–96; *Fort Worth Star Telegram* in, 93; Hispanic population in, 95; legislature in, 93; Republicans and, 95; state capital reporters in, 93; *Texas Monthly* in, 91; voter turnout in, 94. *See also* *Texas Tribune*

Texas Christian University, 148, 151

Texas Monthly, 91

Texas Tribune, 91; editorial page for, 94; funding for, 92; mission of, 91–92, 94. *See also* Smith, Evan

This American Life, 135

Times. See New York Times

Too Embarrassed to Ask, 135

training reporters: college and, 148; editors and, 147

Trump, Donald: on accepting election results, 58; *The Art of the Deal* by, 176, 185; Balz on modern era and, 16; birther rumors and, 57; Bunton on, 149; charity donations of, 176–79; Cillizza story on, 153; CNN coverage of, 109; Colbert as muse for, 141; on defending Japan, 81–82; donation pledges of, 176; election strategy of, 14–15; fake news Tweets by,

161; Fox News coverage of, 14, 109, 172; groping women video with Bush, Billy, and, 181–84; as ideologically unmoored, 17; insults by, 23; on Japan, 81–82; *Journal* on, 85, 86–87; Lewandowski as campaign manager for, 174; on locker room banter, 183; media criticism by, xi, 100, 113; modern era and, 16; money given away by, 172–73, 174–75; on NATO commitment, 81; polling deficit of, 183; pollsters for, 14, 183; portraits of, 178–81; Putin and, 14; on rigged election, 57–58; rural America and, 18; Russia blackmail documents and, 112; on Russian Intelligence Service and Clinton, H., emails, 13; Scarborough on, 17; Seib on victory of, 89; self-dealing of, 179, 180; speaking style of, 7; tax loopholes of, 13; *Times* interviews with, 34; Twitter and, 8; on undocumented immigrants, 18; veteran groups fundraising and, 172–75; Yates fired by, 104. *See also* Donald J. Trump Foundation; Trump administration
Trump, Ivanka, 87–88
Trump administration, xi
Trump foundation. *See* Donald J. Trump Foundation
Turner, Ted, 28
24/7 news cycle: in digital reporting, 152; information overload and, 152, 158

Twitter: African Americans and, 115–16; Bumiller on, 80; BuzzFeed and, 41; Fahrenthold using, 174, 177, 179, 180, 184; fake news and, 59; Trump, D., and, 8
Twitterbots, 55

undocumented immigrants, 18
Uproxx, 49

VandeHei, Jim, 10, 46
The Verge, 49, 125
The Vergecast, 135
veterans groups, 172–75
Vietnam War, 27–28
viral content: BuzzFeed and, 41; fake news and, 55
voter fraud, 58
voter turnout, 94–95
Vox.com, 50
Vox Media, 50; audience of, 39; design for, 40; Recode purchased by, 66. *See also* Bankoff, Jim
VOX The Weeds, 135

Wait Wait . . . Don't Tell Me!, 135
Wallace, Chris, 14, 167; on Fox coverage of Trump, D., 109; as presidential debate moderator, 107
Wall Street Journal (Journal), 31; editorial page of, 86; Mossberg and, 65; Murdock family on Trump, D., reporting in, 85; opinion pages of, 85; podcasts, 135–36; Trump, D., falsehoods and, 86–87; on

Wall Street Journal (continued)
Trump, I., and Kushner rental
from Luksic, 87–88. *See also*
Seib, Gerald
Walter Cronkite era, 105
Washington Post (Post), 163–64;
Balz at, 15; Bezos as new
owner of, 34, 71; campaign
beat reporters at, 76; digital
product for, 8, 10, 72, 73–74;
election win stories at, 185–86;
as media company, 99; opinion
and editorial pages of, 86;
profanity at, 182–83;
readership growth of, 72, 73;

revenue of, 71–72, 77; software
engineers at, 42, 74. *See also*
Baron, Martin; Fahrenthold,
David
Weisman, Jonathan, 80
Weisselberg, Allen, 177
Welch, Edgar, 55–56
What's Tech?, 135
World War II newspapers, 26

Yates, Sally, 104
Youssef, Nancy, 152

Zucker, Jeff, 111–12
Zuckerberg, Mark, 60

About the Authors

BOB SCHIEFFER has spent 48 of his 60 years in journalism at CBS News. He's still working.

H. ANDREW SCHWARTZ is chief communications officer at the Center for Strategic & International Studies and cohost of Bob Schieffer's "About the News" podcast. He was formerly a White House producer at Fox News.

KRISTIE BUNTON holds a PhD from Indiana University and journalism degrees from the University of Missouri. She is dean of the Bob Schieffer College of Communication at Texas Christian University.

LUCY BOYD is on the investigative team at 60 Minutes. She covered the 2016 campaign with Schieffer after earning her master's degree in public policy at Harvard's Kennedy School.

About the Center for Strategic & International Studies

ESTABLISHED IN WASHINGTON, D.C., over 50 years ago, the Center for Strategic & International Studies (CSIS) is a bipartisan, nonprofit policy research organization dedicated to providing strategic insights and policy solutions to help decisionmakers chart a course toward a better world.

In late 2015, Thomas J. Pritzker was named chairman of the CSIS Board of Trustees. Mr. Pritzker succeeded former U.S. senator Sam Nunn (D-GA), who chaired the CSIS Board of Trustees from 1999 to 2015. CSIS is led by John J. Hamre, who has served as president and chief executive officer since 2000.

Founded in 1962 by David M. Abshire and Admiral Arleigh Burke, CSIS is one of the world's preeminent international policy institutions focused on defense and security, regional study, and transnational challenges ranging from energy and trade to global development and economic integration. For the past six years consecutively, CSIS has been named the world's number one think tank for international security by the University of Pennsylvania's "Go To Think Tank Index."

The Center's 220 full-time staff and large network of affiliated scholars conduct research and analysis and develop policy initiatives that look to the future and anticipate change. CSIS is regularly called upon by Congress, the executive branch, and the media to explain the day's events and offer bipartisan recommendations to improve U.S. strategy.

CSIS does not take specific policy positions; accordingly, all views expressed herein should be understood to be solely those of the author(s).